Books by George Steiner

EXTRA-
TERRITORIAL

GEORGE STEINER

EXTRA-
TERRITORIAL

Papers on Literature
and the Language
Revolution

ATHENEUM   NEW YORK
1976

The following articles appeared originally in *The New Yorker:* "Of Nuance and Scruple," "Tigers in the Mirror," "Cry Havoc," "A Death of Kings," "Tongues of Men" and "Life-Lines." "Extraterritorial" and "Linguistics and Poetics" first appeared in *Tri-Quarterly*. "The Language Animal" first appeared in *Encounter*. "In a Post-Culture" first appeared in *The Times Literary Supplement*.

For Ivor and Dorothy Richards

FOREWORD

I t is a commonplace to note that there has been a "language revolution." The idea that the coding and transmission of ordered information is crucial to the definition of man is now focal, not only in philosophy, in logic, in social theory, and in the study of the arts, but also as a central presence in the life sciences. The intense energies of spirit, the technical force which linguistics has shown over these past decades are both the stimulus and the consequence of a larger re-direction. The articles and papers put together in this book deal with related aspects of this general movement. They consider certain philosophic and literary elements in this radical return—a renovation which is at the same time a re-experiencing—of the image of the human person as uniquely related to the act of speech, to the Logos.

The sources of the language revolution coincide in time and sensibility with that crisis of morals and of formal values which immediately precedes and follows on the First World War, particularly in Central Europe. What I have called elsewhere "the retreat from the word" and the failure of humane literacy in the face of barbarism directly counterpoints the new linguistics, the new attempts—philosophical, psychological, poetic—to establish a semantic center. At several places in this collection, I try to indicate some of the lines of internal relation and reciprocity between the linguistic analyses of the early Russell and Wittgenstein, the investigations of the Moscow and Prague language circles, and the trope of silence or failed speech in the literature of Hofmannsthal, Kafka, and the moderns. Analytic and mimetic ways of experiencing the deep paradoxality and fragility of language interact at numerous key points. Wittgenstein's *Tractatus* has its substantive counterpart in the poetry, drama, and even music of the period. This set of articles is a preliminary essay toward a history of the change in speech awareness, of the change in the ways culture inhabits language, as it has occurred since the 1890's.

A striking aspect of this language revolution has been the emergence of linguistic pluralism or "unhousedness" in certain great writers. These writers stand in a relation of dialectical hesitance not only toward one native tongue —as Hölderlin or Rimbaud did before them—but toward several languages. This is almost unprecedented. It speaks of the more general problem of a lost center. It makes of Nabokov, Borges, and Beckett the three representative figures in the literature of exile—which is, perhaps, the main impulse of current literature. Different papers in this book touch on one or another aspect of their extraterritoriality. Only the article on Céline goes back to my earlier work, to my attempts to locate more precisely the coexistence of political barbarism with literary merit.

To focus on the linguistic elements in Nabokov or Beckett, on the inter- and intra-linguistic cat's cradle of their inventions, is an obvious move. But it points to the more general theme of the effects of the language revolution on the ways in which we read literature. These effects seem to me penetrating and provocative. The demands made of literary criticism by Roman Jakobson and the poet-linguists of the Moscow Language Circle now press on literary awareness—or should be felt to do so—with a new insistence. All literature is a linguistic construct. The philosophic, logical-linguistic, psychological investigations of syntax and of the grammars of human feeling, as they have been conducted since 1900, cannot be irrelevant to literature. On the contrary: the poetic case is the essential, the ontologically crystallized instance, of the life of language. The precise authority and range of pertinence which linguistics has for the poet, the student of letters, and the common reader remain arguable, and rightly so. But the argument must be pressed home if literary criticism and literary history are again to become a serious enterprise (they are hardly that at the moment). At the pivot of this collection stands a paper which seeks to state what ought to be the creative interactions between linguistics and poetics.

Today, any thinking about the nature of language and the relations of language to mind will have to take up either the whole of transformational generative linguistics or, at least, those sections of the model nearest its own concerns. This is as it should be. The contributions of Noam Chomsky to the formalization of the theory of grammar, and to the place now held by that theory in the study of logic and psychology, are pre-eminent. These are, moreover, contributions of great elegance and intellectual fascination. I am neither competent nor inclined to question their technical value and coherence. They are already, and decidedly, a classic part of the history of linguistic investigation. My differences with Chomskian linguistics—differences argued throughout this book—are of a more fundamental kind.

I am persuaded that the phenomenon of language is such that a rigorously idealized and nearly mathematical account of the deep structures and generation of human speech is bound to be incomplete and, very possibly, distorting. It is the thinness, the determinism of the generative transformational case—particularly in its current dogmatic vein—that I find disturbing. It is the refusal to see at how immediate a level problems of formal description become a matter of general philosophy and of the image one has of man's relations to the Logos.

In part, this is a point of history. Despite its references to the grammarians of Port Royal and to Humboldt, Chomskian linguistics is insistent, often polemically, on its innovative autonomy. It is also rigorous in its inference of what is or is not relevant, of what is or is not respectable. The latter exclusion is key: in it, the intense ambition to be thought a "science" is constantly operative. This has meant not only a damaging failure to take just account of a good deal of the philosophic-linguistic work of Saussure (from whom, as it happens, the entire competence/performance distinction stems), of Wittgenstein, and of I. A. Richards, but a total indifference to the more speculative, meta-logical areas of the philosophy of language.

I have in mind the phenomenological tradition of Dilthey and Husserl with its stress on the historicity of speech acts, on the time-boundedness and mutations of even the most elemental of semantic modes. I am thinking of the investigations into language by Heidegger, of Paul Ricoeur's *De l'Interprétation*, and of the whole hermeneutic approach now so lively in France, Italy, and Germany. Or of the school of exegesis gathered around the Austrian journal the *Brenner*, immediately before and after 1914–18, with its emphasis on the religious, "pneumatological" characteristics of human speech, and its links, as yet to be studied, with the early Wittgenstein. Cut off from these philosophic traditions, contemptuous of the uncertainties and transcendental intimations which they enact, the new linguistics, with its declared meta-mathematical ideals, runs the risk of a powerful triviality. (I include a small piece on chess in this book not only because of its obvious relevance to Nabokov, but to illustrate closely the notion of a mental construct which is at once powerful and formally of extreme depth, but also essentially trivial.) The peremptory naïvetés of a good deal of transformational generative work make impossible any real access to language when it is in a condition of maximal concentration, when, as Heidegger says, language is total being, i.e., to literature. A scientific dogmatism (is there, in fact, a "linguistic science"?) would exclude from rational inquiry the "mystery" of language, its median state between spirituality and physical articulation. Yet it is in that median quality, and in the fact, as Quine states it, that "No two of us learn our language alike, nor, in a sense, does any finish learning it while he lives," that may be sought primary clues to the linguistic core of human identity.

The theme of Babel is a case in point. The "counter-economic" development on a crowded earth of many thousands of mutually incomprehensible tongues, often set only miles apart, poses fundamental problems. A comprehensive theory of language—which will also be a theory of man's singular humanity—cannot dismiss the question as pertaining merely to surface features. It is not in transformational grammars, however, but in hermeneutics, in the *Sprachphilosophie* of Walter Benjamin, with its unashamed roots in kabbalistic thought, that the implications of Babel are grasped. The points at which I touch on the Babel motif in these articles are preliminary to a full-length study.

Professor Chomsky has expressed strong doubts to me as to whether linguistics and the biological sciences have anything of value to say to each other. He may well be proved right. Nevertheless, at present the exchanges of terminology, of implicit models, of habits of understanding, are vivid. They mark both fields, making of them, as it were, branches of a comprehensive science of meaning. Even if it should turn out that the affinities have been only metaphoric, such mirrorings through metaphor are of intense concern to the history of culture. I look at some of these reciprocities in the closing essay.

But my argument is also a more general one. The "incorporation" of the mental energies and speculative forms of the sciences—the incarnation of the zest and beauty of these forms—into educated literacy, into the normal life of the imagination, is a dominant issue in what is left of our culture. That incorporation must be attempted, even where it will remain largely "imaged" or analogized, if we are to emerge from the drift and boredom of semi-literacy. One of the papers in this collection addresses itself specifically to this theme. Again, I believe, there is no inevitable merit in rejecting the religious or metaphysical reaches of the argument. For to speak of the generation and condition of language is to speak of that of man.

G. S.

Yale University
October, 1970

CONTENTS

EXTRA-TERRITORIAL

EXTRATERRITORIAL

Romantic theory argues that, of all men, the writer most obviously incarnates the genius, *Geist*, quiddity of his native speech. Each language crystallizes the inner history, the specific world-view of the *Volk* or nation. This theory is a natural part of romantic historicism and the nineteenth-century discovery of the shaping power of linguistic development. Indo-European philology seemed not only a road into the otherwise unrecapturable past, into the time of the roots of consciousness, but also a uniquely penetrative approach to the matter of ethnic quality. These notions, eloquent in Herder, Michelet, Humboldt, seem to match common sense. The writer is a special master of the language. In him the energies of idiomatic usage, of etymological implication, declare themselves with obvious force. He may, as D. W. Harding says in a well-known passage, bring "language to bear on the incipient thought at an earlier stage of its development" than do ordinary speakers. But it is *his* language he brings to bear; it is his familiarity with it, somnambular, genetic, that makes the bearing radical and inventive. The life of the language, in turn, reflects the writer's presence more than it does that of any other *métier:* "We must be free or die, who speak the tongue/That Shakespeare spake."

Hence the *a priori* strangeness of the idea of a writer linguistically "unhoused," of a poet, novelist, playwright

3

not thoroughly at home in the language of his production, but displaced or hesitant at the frontier. Yet this sense of strangeness is more recent than one might think. Much of European vulgate literature has behind it the active pressure of more than one language. I would argue that a good deal of poetry from Petrarch to Hölderlin is "classical" in a very material sense: it represents a long act of *imitatio*, an inner translation into the relevant vernacular of Greek and Latin modes of statement and feeling. Literal currents of Greek, Latin, and Italian move through Milton's English. Racine's perfect economy depends, in part, on the completing echo of the passage from Euripides—an echo fully present in the poet's mind and assumed to be so, in some degree at least, in that of his literate public. Bilingualism, in the sense of an equal expressive fluency in one's own language and in Latin and/or French, was the rule rather than the exception among the European *élite* until the latter eighteenth century. Quite often, in fact, the writer felt more at ease in Latin or in French than he did in his own tongue: Alfieri's memoirs tell of his long struggle to acquire natural authority in Italian. Latin poetry continued to be produced until almost our own time.

Nevertheless, there is more than nationalist mystique to the notion of the writer *enraciné*. Latin was, after all, a very special case, a sacramental and cultural interlingua preserving its function precisely because the European vernaculars were moving apart in deepening self-consciousness. The language of Shakespeare, of Montaigne, of Luther, embodies an extreme local strength, an assertion of specific, "untranslatable" identity. For the writer to become bi- or multi-lingual in the modern way, genuine shifts of sensibility and personal status had to occur. These are visible, for the first time perhaps, in Heine. Binary values characterize his life. He was a Jew with a Christian upbringing and a Voltairian view of both traditions. His poetry modulates continually between a romantic-conservative and a radical, satiric stress. Politics and personal mood

4

made him a commuter in Europe. This condition determined his equal currency in French and in German and gave to his German poetry a particular genius. "The fluency and clarity which Heine appropriated from current speech," says T. W. Adorno, "is the very opposite of native 'at-homeness' (*Geborgenheit*). Only he who is not truly at home inside a language uses it as an instrument." The bilingual ambitions of Oscar Wilde may have had even subtler roots. There is the Anglo-Irish relation with its traditional bias toward an eccentric, exhibitionist mastery over English; there is also the Irish use of France as a counter to English values and Wilde's own use of French thought and writing to strengthen his aesthetic, liberating polemics against Victorian standards. But I wonder whether the linguistic display which allowed Wilde to write *Salomé* in French (or which inspired the Latin verse of Lionel Johnson) does not point deeper. We know absurdly little about the vital congruence of eros and language. Oscar Wilde's bilingualism may be an expressive enactment of sexual duality, a speech-symbol for the new rights of experiment and instability he claimed for the life of the artist. Here, as at other important points, Wilde is one of the true sources of the modern tone.

The links with Samuel Beckett are obvious. Another Irishman, fantastically proficient in both French and English, rootless because so variously at home. For a good deal of Beckett's work we do not know whether the English or the French version came first. His parallel texts have an uncanny brilliance. Both language currents seem simultaneously active in Beckett's inter- and intra-lingual composition; translating his own jokes, puns, acrostics, he seems to find in the other language the unique, natural analogue. It is as if the initial job of invention was done in a crypto-language, compounded equally of French, English, Anglo-Irish, and totally private phonemes. Though he does not, so far as I know, publish poetry or parables outside Spanish, Borges is another of the new "esperantists." His intimacy

5

with French, German, and, particularly, with English is profound. Very often an English text—Blake, Stevenson, Coleridge, De Quincey—underlies the Spanish statement. The other language "shines through," giving to Borges' verse and to his *Fictions* a quality of lightness, of universality. He uses the vulgate and mythology of Argentina to ballast what might otherwise be almost too abstract, too peregrine an imagination.

As it happens, these multilinguists (Ezra Pound has his place in this context) are among the foremost writers of the age. The equation of a single pivot of language, of native deep-rootedness, with poetic authority is again in doubt. And, if we except Latin, perhaps in real doubt for the first time. This is a decisive aspect of Nabokov.

The Nabokov bibliography is full of traps and obscurities. But it seems established that he has produced original work in at least three languages. I say "at least" because it may be that one story, "O.," taken up in *Speak, Memory* (1951) and later in *Nabokov's Dozen* (1958), first appeared under the same title, in French, in *Mesures* (Paris, 1939).

This is only one facet of Nabokov's multilingual nature. His translations, re-translations, pastiches, cross-linguistic imitations, etc., form a dizzying cat's-cradle. No bibliographer has, until now, fully unraveled it. Nabokov has translated poems of Ronsard, Verlaine, Supervielle, Baudelaire, Musset, Rimbaud from French into Russian. Nabokov has translated the following English and Irish poets into Russian: Rupert Brooke, Seumas O'Sullivan, Tennyson, Yeats, Byron, Keats, and Shakespeare. His Russian version of *Alice in Wonderland* (Berlin, 1923) has long been recognized as one of the keys to the whole Nabokovian *œuvre*. Among Russian writers whom Nabokov has translated into French and English are Lermontov, Tiutchev, Afanasi Fet, and the Anonymous of *The Song of Igor's Campaign*. His *Eugene Onegin*, in four volumes with mammoth textual apparatus and commentary, may prove to be his (perverse) *magnum opus*. Nabokov has published a Russian text of the Prologue to Goethe's *Faust*. One of his most bizarre feats is a re-translation back into English of Konstantin Bal'mont's "wretched but famous" (Andrew Field: *Nabokov*, p. 372) Russian version of Edgar Allan Poe's *The Bells*. Shades of Borges' Pierre Menard!

Equally important as, if not more so than, these translations, mimes, canonic inversions, and pastiches of other writers—darting to and fro between Russian, French, German, English, and American—are Nabokov's multilingual recastings of Nabokov. Not only is he, together with his son Dimitri Nabokov, the principal translator into English of his own early Russian novels and tales, but he has translated (?) *Lolita* back (?) into Russian, and there are those who consider this version, published in New York in 1967, to be the novelist's crowning deed.

I have no hesitation in arguing that this polylinguistic matrix is the determining fact of Nabokov's life and art, or, as Field more aptly phrases it, "life in art." Nabokov's passions for entomology (a branch of the theory of classification) and chess—particularly chess problems—are "meta-linguistic" parallels to his principal obsession. This obsession is, of course, not wholly of Nabokov's choosing. As he points out with tireless, aggrieved insistence, the political barbarism of the century made him an exile, a wanderer, a *Hotelmensch*, not only from his Russian homeland but from the matchless Russian tongue in which his genius would have found its unforced idiom. This is obviously the case. But, whereas so many other language exiles clung desperately to the artifice of their native tongue or fell silent, Nabokov moved into successive languages like a traveling potentate. Banished from Fialta, he has built for himself a house of words. To be specific: the multilingual, cross-linguistic situation is both the matter and form of Nabokov's work (the two are, no doubt, inseparable and *Pale Fire* is the parable of their fusion).

It would be by no means eccentric to read the major part

7

of Nabokov's opus as a meditation—lyric, ironic, technical, parodistic—on the nature of human language, on the enigmatic coexistence of different, linguistically generated world visions and of a deep current underlying, and at moments obscurely conjoining, the multitude of diverse tongues. *The Gift, Lolita,* and *Ada* are tales of the erotic relations between speaker and speech and, more precisely, laments, often as formal and plangent as the funeral orations of the baroque, for Nabokov's separation from the one true beloved, "my Russian language." It is with two other masters of that language, Pushkin and Gogol, and with his predecessor in exile, Bunin, that Nabokov feels himself to be essentially contemporary. The theme haunts *Speak, Memory,* to me the most humane and modest of Nabokov's books. It comes through penetratingly even in the more didactic, explicitly technical of Nabokov's pronouncements. As he told his Wellesley students in 1945, "You can, and should, speak Russian with a permanent broad smile." In Russian, a vowel is an orange, in English a mere lemon. This also, I would judge, is the source of the motif of incest, so prevalent throughout Nabokov's fiction and central to *Ada.* Incest is a trope through which Nabokov dramatizes his abiding devotion to Russian, the dazzling infidelities which exile has forced on him, and the unique intimacy he has achieved with his own writings as begetter, translator, and re-translator. Mirrors, incest, and a constant meshing of languages are the cognate centers of Nabokov's art.

This leads, inevitably, to the question of "Nabokese," the Anglo-American interlingua in which Nabokov has produced the bulk of his work since the early 1940's. There are those who regard the language of *Lolita* and its successors as a wonder of invention, elegance, and wit. To other ears, Nabokov's prose is a macaronic, precious, maddeningly opaque and self-conscious piece of candy floss. It is alien not only in details of lexical usage, but in its primary rhythms, which go against the natural grain of

English and American speech. In the main, this kind of disagreement is a matter of olives: one has the taste or one doesn't. At a first reading, *Ada* (in so many ways a variation on the themes of *Pale Fire*) seems self-indulgent and, at many points, irredeemably overwritten. The Newspeak of Ardor is often on the same predictable level of ingenuity as double acrostics. The mixture of English, French, Russian, and private esperanto is labored. It is as if Nabokov had been mastered by that multilingual dilemma which has, until now, been so notably in his control. But, with a writer of this reach, first readings are always inadequate. Lived with, the layer cake in *Ada* may prove a culinary find. It is, I feel, less profitable at this stage to debate over the merits or vices of "Nabokese" than it is to throw light on its sources and fabric.

We need really detailed study of the quality and degree of pressure which Russian puts on Nabokov's Anglo-American. How often are his English sentences "meta-translations" of Russian? To what extent do Russian semantic associations initiate the images and contour of the English phrase? Especially, we need an authoritative concordance of Nabokov's Russian poetry and English prose. I suspect that many of the characteristic motions of style in Nabokov's fiction since *Sebastian Knight* embody a resurrection of, or variation on, the poetry which Nabokov produced in Russian from 1914 to 1939. Whole episodes in *Lolita* and *Ada*, as well as the Augustan mock-epic pastiche in *Pale Fire*, appear to have precise roots in Russian poems, some of which go back to the early 1920's. Is a good deal of Nabokov's English a piece of smuggling, an illicit conveyance across the frontier, of Russian verse now captive in a society he contemns?

We also require careful analysis of the local and literary background of Nabokov's English. Its aesthetics, its particular rhetoric, the ideals of exact profusion and ironic pedantry it aims at, can be placed. We find them in the Cambridge which Nabokov attended as an undergraduate,

9

and in related Bloomsbury. Allowing for all that the book owes to Gogol, I find it difficult to dissociate *Lolita* from the English versions of *art nouveau*, from the colorations of Beardsley, Wilde, and Firbank. The lordly asperities and *glissandos* of condescension which are so distinctive of the Nabokov tone can be paralleled in Lytton Strachey, Max Beerbohm, and the early Evelyn Waugh. Indeed, the whole stance of the amateur/*amatore* of genius, fastidiously at ease in a dozen branches of arcane learning, always turning toward the golden afternoons and vintages of the past, is demonstrably late Edwardian and Georgian. That Nabokov's earliest translations and vignettes should concern Rupert Brooke and Cambridge is indicative. Much in his art, and much that now seems most idiosyncratic or original, is a re-invention of that lost world of white flannels and honey for tea. In the England of Virginia Woolf, Nabokov found interwoven the two principal "topics" of his sensibility: the lilac summers of a lost, aristocratic order, and the erotic ambiguities of Lewis Carroll. One would want to know also what forms of American vulgate and American literature (if he read any) bore in on Nabokov after 1941.

All these would be preliminary lines of inquiry toward getting right the "strangeness," the polysemic nature of Nabokov's uses of language[s]. They would clarify not only his own prodigious talent, but such larger questions as the condition of multilingual imagining, of internalized translation, of the possible existence of a private mixed idiom "beneath," "coming before" the localization of different languages in the articulate brain. Like Borges— whom he cheaply and self-betrayingly mocks in *Ada*— Nabokov is a writer who works very near the intricate threshold of syntax; he experiences linguistic forms in a state of manifold potentiality and, moving across vernaculars, is able to keep words and phrases in a charged, unstable mode of vitality. Beyond the personal case, moreover, we find the representative stance, or, rather, motion.

A great writer driven from language to language by social upheaval and war is an apt symbol for the age of the refugee. No exile is more radical, no feat of adaptation and new life more demanding. It seems proper that those who create art in a civilization of quasi-barbarism which has made so many homeless, which has torn up tongues and peoples by the root, should themselves be poets unhoused and wanderers across language. Eccentric, aloof, nostalgic, deliberately untimely as he aspires to be and so often is, Nabokov remains, by virtue of his extraterritoriality, profoundly of our time, and one of its spokesmen.

OF NUANCE AND SCRUPLE

At certain times in literature, a particular writer seems to embody the dignity and solitude of the entire profession. Henry James was "the Master" not only or even mainly by virtue of his gifts but because his manner of life, his style, even on trivial occasions, expressed the compulsive ministry of great art. Today there is reason to suppose that Samuel Beckett is the writer par excellence, that other playwrights and novelists find in him the concentrated shadow of their strivings and privations. Monsieur Beckett is—to the last fiber of his compact, elusive being—*métier*. There is no discernible waste motion, no public flourish, no concession—or none that is heralded—to the noise and imprecisions of life. Beckett's early years have an air of deliberate apprenticeship (he was at the age of twenty-one acting as secretary to Joyce). His first publications, the essay on "Dante . . . Bruno . . . Vico . . . Joyce" of 1929, the 1931 monograph on Proust, a collection of poems issued in 1935 by the Europa Press—a name symptomatic—are exact preliminaries. Beckett charts, in regard to his own needs, the proximate attractions of Joyce and Proust; he is most influenced by what he discards. In *More Pricks Than Kicks* (London, 1934), he strikes his own special note. War came as a banal interruption. It surrounded Beckett with a silence, a routine of lunacy and sorrow as tangible as that already guessed at in his art.

12

With *Molloy* in 1951 and *Waiting for Godot*, a year later, Beckett achieved that least interesting but most necessary of conditions—timeliness. Time had caught up; the major artist is, precisely, one who dreams ahead.

Henry James was representative through the stately profusion of his work, through the conviction, manifest in all he wrote, that language, if pursued with enough fastidious energy, could be made to realize and convey the sum of worthwhile experience. Beckett's sparsity, his genius for saying less, is the antithesis. Beckett uses words as if each had to be extracted from a safe and smuggled into the light from a stock dangerously low. If the same word will do, use it many times over, until it is rubbed fine and anonymous. Breath is a legacy not to be squandered; monosyllables are enough for weekdays. Praised be the saints for full stops; they keep us prodigal babblers from penury. The notion that we can express to our deaf selves, let alone communicate to any other human beings, blind, deaf, insensate as they are, a complete truth, fact, sensation—a fifth, tenth, millionth of such aforesaid truth, fact, or sensation—is arrogant folly. James clearly believed the thing was feasible; so did Proust, and Joyce when, in a last, crazy spree, he flung a net of bright, sounding words over all of creation. Now the park gates are shut, top hats and rhetoric molder on empty benches. Saints above, sir, it's hard enough for a man to get up stairs, let alone *say* so:

> There were not many steps. I had counted them a thousand times, both going up and coming down, but the figure has gone from my mind. I have never known whether you should say one with your foot on the sidewalk, two with the following foot on the first step, and so on, or whether the sidewalk shouldn't count. At the top of the steps I fell foul of the same dilemma. In the other direction, I mean from top to bottom, it was the same, the word is not too strong. I did not know where to begin nor where to end, that's

the truth of the matter. I arrived therefore at three totally different figures, without ever knowing which of them was right. And when I say that the figure has gone from my mind, I mean that none of the three figures is with me any more, in my mind.

Beckett's *reductio* of language—*Echo's Bones*, the title of his early book of verse, is a perfect designation—relates to much that is distinctive of modern feeling. "It was the same, the word is not too strong" exhibits the tense playfulness of linguistic philosophy. There are passages in Beckett nearly interchangeable with the "language exercises" in Wittgenstein's *Investigations;* both stalk the vapid inflations and imprecisions of our common speech. *Act Without Words* (1957) is to drama what *Black on Black* is to painting, a display of reductive logic. Beckett's silences, his wry assumption that a rose may indeed be a rose but that only a fool would take so scandalous a proposition for granted or feel confident of translating it into art, are akin to monochrome canvases, Warhol statics, and silent music.

But with a difference. There is in Beckett a formidable inverse eloquence. Words, hoarded and threadbare as they are, dance for him as they do for all Irish bards. Partly this is a matter of repetition made musical; partly it springs from a cunning delicacy of to and fro, a rhythm of exchange closely modeled on slapstick. Beckett has links with Gertrude Stein and Kafka. But it is from the Marx Brothers that Vladimir and Estragon or Hamm and Clov have learned most. There are fugues of dialogue in *Waiting for Godot*—although "dialogue," with its implication of efficient contact, is painfully the wrong word—that come nearest in current literature to pure rhetoric:

> VLADIMIR: We have our reasons.
> ESTRAGON: All the dead voices.
> VLADIMIR: They make a noise like wings.
> ESTRAGON: Like leaves.

14

VLADIMIR: Like sand.
ESTRAGON: Like leaves.
Silence
VLADIMIR: They all speak at once.
ESTRAGON: Each one to itself.
Silence
VLADIMIR: Rather they whisper.
ESTRAGON: They rustle.
VLADIMIR: They murmur.
ESTRAGON: They rustle.
Silence
VLADIMIR: What do they say?
ESTRAGON: They talk about their lives.
VLADIMIR: To have lived is not enough for them.
ESTRAGON: They have to talk about it.
VLADIMIR: To be dead is not enough for them.
ESTRAGON: It is not sufficient.
Silence
VLADIMIR: They make a noise like feathers.
ESTRAGON: Like leaves.
VLADIMIR: Like ashes.
ESTRAGON: Like leaves.
Long silence

A topic for future dissertations: uses of silence in Webern and Beckett. In *Textes pour Rien* (1955), we learn that we simply cannot go on speaking of souls and bodies, of births, lives, and deaths; we must carry on without any of that as best we can. "All that is the death of words, all that is superfluity of words, they do not know how to say anything else, but will say it no more." I look, says Beckett, "for the voice of my silence." The silences that punctuate his discourse, whose differing lengths and intensities seem as carefully modulated as they are in music, are not empty. They have in them, almost audible, the echo of things unspoken. And, especially, of words said in another language.

15

Samuel Beckett is master of two languages. This is a new and deeply suggestive phenomenon. Until very recently, a writer has been, almost by definition, a being rooted in his native idiom, a sensibility housed more closely, more inevitably, than ordinary men and women in the shell of one language. To be a good writer signified a special intimacy with the rhythms of speech that lie deeper than formal syntax; it meant having an ear for those multitudinous connotations and buried echoes of an idiom no dictionary can convey. A poet or novelist whom political exile or private disaster had cut off from his native speech was a creature maimed.

Oscar Wilde was one of the first modern "dualists" (the qualification is necessary because bilingualism in Latin and one's own vulgate was, of course, a general condition of high culture in medieval and Renaissance Europe). Wilde wrote in French, but uncertainly, to display the rootless elegance and irony toward fixed counters that marked his entire work and career. Kafka experienced the simultaneous pressures and poetic temptations of three languages—Czech, German, and Yiddish. A number of his tales and parables can be read as symbolic confessions by a man not fully domiciled in the language in which he chose, or found himself compelled, to write. Kafka notes in his diary for 24th October, 1911:

> Yesterday it occurred to me that I did not always love my mother as she deserved and as I could, only because the German language prevented it. The Jewish mother is no "Mutter," to call her "Mutter" makes her a little comic. . . . For the Jew, "Mutter" is specifically German. . . . The Jewish woman who is called "Mutter" therefore becomes not only comic but strange.

But the writer as linguistic polymath, as actively at home in several languages, is something very new. That the three figures of probable genius in contemporary fiction

—Nabokov, Borges, and Beckett—should each have a virtuoso fluency in several languages, that Nabokov and Beckett should have produced major works in two or more utterly different tongues, is a fact of enormous interest. Its implications so far as the new internationalism of culture goes have hardly been grasped. Their performance and, to a lesser degree, that of Ezra Pound—with its deliberate sandwiching of languages and alphabets—suggest that the modernist movement can be seen as a strategy of permanent exile. The artist and the writer are incessant tourists window-shopping over the entire compass of available forms. The conditions of linguistic stability, of local, national self-consciousness in which literature flourished between the Renaissance and, say, the 1950's are now under extreme stress. Faulkner and Dylan Thomas might one day be seen as among the last major "homeowners" of literature. Joyce's employment at Berlitz and Nabokov's residence in a Swiss hotel may come to stand as signs for the age. Increasingly, every act of communication between human beings takes on the shape of an act of translation.

In order to grasp Beckett's parallel, mutually informing virtuosity, two aids are necessary: the critical bibliography gathered by Raymond Federman and John Fletcher (*Samuel Beckett: His Works and His Critics*, University of California Press) and the trilingual edition of Beckett's plays issued by Suhrkamp Verlag in Frankfurt in 1963–64. Roughly until 1945, Beckett wrote in English; after that, he composed mainly in French. But the situation is complicated by the fact that *Watt* (1953) has so far appeared only in English and by the constant possibility that work published in French was first written in English, and vice versa. *Waiting for Godot, Endgame, Molloy, Malone Dies, The Unnamable*, and the recent *Têtes Mortes* first appeared in French. Most of these texts, but not all, have been translated by Beckett into English (were some of them conceived in English?), usually with alterations and

17

excisions. Beckett's bibliography is as labyrinthine as Nabokov's or as some of the multilingual *œuvres* Borges lists in his *Fictions*. The same book or fragment may lead several lives; pieces go underground and reappear much later, subtly transmuted. To study Beckett's genius seriously, one must lay side by side the French and English versions of *Waiting for Godot* or *Malone Dies*, in which the French version most probably has preceded the English, then do the same with *All That Fall* or *Happy Days*, in which Beckett reverses himself and recasts his English text into French. After which, quite in the vein of a Borges fable, one ought to rotate the eight texts around a common center to follow the permutations of Beckett's wit and sensibility within the matrix of two great tongues. Only in this way can one make out to what degree Beckett's idiom—the laconic, arch, delicately paced inflections of his style—is a *pas de deux* of French and English, with a strong dose of Irish tomfoolery and arcane sadness added.

Such is Beckett's dual control that he translates his own jokes by altering them, by finding in his alternative language an exact counterpart to the undertones, idiomatic associations, or social context of the original. No outside translator would have chosen the equivalences found by Beckett for the famous crescendo of mutual flyting in Act II of *Waiting for Godot*. "*Andouille! Tordu! Crétin! Curé! Dégueulasse! Micheton! Ordure! Archi . . . tecte!*" is not translated, in any ordinary sense, by "Moron! Vermin! Abortion! Morpion! Sewerrat! Curate! Cretin! Crritic!" "Morpion" is a delicate borrowing from the French, signifying both a kind of flea and a game analogous to Vladimir's and Estragon's alignment of insults, but a borrowing *not* from the French text initially provided by Beckett himself! The accelerando of outrage conveyed by the *cr*-sounds in the English version springs from the French not by translation but by intimate re-creation; Beckett seems capable of reliving in either French or English the poetic, associative processes that produced his initial text. Thus, to compare

18

Lucky's crazed monologue in its French and English casts is to be given a memorable lesson in the singular genius of both languages as well as in their European interaction. A wealth of sly precision lies behind the "translation" of Seine-et-Oise, Seine-et-Marne into Feckham Peckham Fulham Clapham. The death of Voltaire becomes, appropriately, yet with a distinct shift of stress, that of Dr. Johnson. Not even Connemara stays put; it suffers a sea change into *"Normandie on ne sait pourquoi."*

Stories and Texts for Nothing (1968) is a case in point. This collection of three short fables and thirteen monologues is a cat's-cradle. The stories seem to have been written in French in 1945 and are related to both *Molloy* and *Malone Dies.* The monologues and stories appeared in Paris in 1955, but at least one had already been published in a magazine. The English edition of this book, under the title of *No's Knife, Collected Shorter Prose,* includes four items not included in the American version, among them "Ping," a weird miniature. The New York edition is, as has been noted elsewhere, no compliment to Beckett's austere pedantry in matters of dating and bibliography. The few indications given are erroneous or incomplete. This is a fascinating but minor work. Slight if only because Beckett allows a number of influences or foreign bodies to obtrude. Jonathan Swift, always a ghostly precedent, looms large in the dirt and hallucinations of "The End." There is more Kafka, or, rather, more undisguised Kafka, than Beckett usually permits one to detect: "That's where the court sits this evening, in the depths of that vaulty night, that's where I'm clerk and scribe, not understanding what I hear, not knowing what I write." Joyce is very much with us, Irish ballad, end of winter's day, horsecab and all, in "The Expelled." We read in "The Calmative" that "there was never any city but the one" and are meant to grasp a twofold unity, Dublin-Paris, the venue of the great artificer and now of Beckett himself.

But although these are fragments, four-finger exercises,

19

the essential motifs come through. The spirit shuffles like a ragpicker in quest of words that have not been chewed to the marrow, that have kept something of their secret life despite the mendacity of the age. The dandy as ascetic, the fastidious beggar—these are Beckett's natural personae. The keynote is one of genuine yet faintly insolent amazement: "It's enough to make you wonder sometimes if you are on the right planet. Even the words desert you, it's as bad as that." The apocalypse is a death of speech (which echoes the rhetorical but no less final desolation of *King Lear*):

All the peoples of the earth would not suffice, at the end of the billions you'd need a god, unwitnessed witness of witnesses, what a blessing it's all down the drain, nothing ever as much as begun, nothing ever but nothing and never, nothing ever but lifeless words.

Yet sometimes in this kingdom of ashcans and rain "words were coming back to me, and the way to make them sound."

When that pentecostal dispensation lights, Beckett literally sings, in a low, penetrating voice, cunning in its cadence. Beckett's style makes other contemporary prose seem flatulent:

I know what I mean, or one-armed better still, no arms, no hands, better by far, as old as the world and no less hideous, amputated on all sides, erect on my trusty stumps, bursting with . . . old prayers, old lessons, soul, mind, and carcass finishing neck and neck, not to mention the gobchucks, too painful to mention, sobs made mucus, hawked up from the heart, now I have a heart, now I'm complete. . . . Evenings, evenings, what evenings they were then, made of what, and when was that, I don't know, made of friendly shadows, friendly skies, of time cloyed, resting from devouring, until its midnight meats, I

20

don't know, any more than then, when I used to say, from within, or from without, from the coming night or from under the ground.

The laconic wit of "soul, mind, and carcass finishing neck and neck" would by itself signal the hand of a major poet. But the entirety of this eleventh monologue or murmuring meditation is high poetry, and seeks out Shakespeare with distant, teasing echo ("where I am, between two parting dreams, knowing none, known of none").

Beckett's landscape is a bleak monochrome. The matter of his singsong is ordure, solitude, and the ghostly self-sufficiency that comes after a long fast. Nevertheless, he is one of our indispensable recorders, and knows it, too: "Peekaboo here I come again, just when most needed, like the square root of minus one, having terminated my humanities." A dense, brilliantly apt phrase. The square root of minus one is imaginary, spectral, but mathematics cannot do without it. "Terminated" is a deliberate gallicism: it signifies that Beckett has mastered humane learning (these texts bristle with arcane allusions), that he has made an academic inventory of civilization before closing the lid and paring himself to the bone. But "terminated" also means finis, Endgame, Krapp's Last Tape. This is terminal art, making most criticism or commentary a superfluous vulgarity.

The vision that emerges from the sum of Beckett's writings is narrow and repetitive. It is also hilarious. It may not be much, but, being so honest, it might well prove the best, most durable we have. Beckett's thinness, his refusal to see in language and literary form adequate realizations of human feeling or society, make him antithetical to Henry James. But he is as representative of our present diminished reach as James was representative of a lost spaciousness. There applies to both the salutation spoken by W. H. Auden in Mount Auburn cemetery: "Master of nuance and scruple."

21

TIGERS IN THE MIRROR

Inevitably, the current world fame of Jorge Luis Borges entails a sense of private loss. As when a view long treasured—the shadow-mass of Arthur's Seat in Edinburgh seen, uniquely, from the back of number sixty The Pleasance, or Fifty-first Street in Manhattan angled to a bronze and racing canyon through a trick of elevation and light in my dentist's window—a collector's item of and for the inner eye, becomes a panoptic spectacle for the tourist horde. For a long time, the splendor of Borges was clandestine, signaled to the happy few, bartered in undertones and mutual recognitions. How many knew of his first work, a summary of Greek myths, written in English in Buenos Aires, the author aged seven? Or of opus two, dated 1907 and distinctly premonitory, a translation into Spanish of Oscar Wilde's *The Happy Prince?* To affirm today that "Pierre Menard, Author of the Quixote" is one of the sheer wonders of human contrivance, that the several facets of Borges' shy genius are almost wholly gathered in that spare fable, is a platitude. But how many own the *editio princeps* of *El jardin de senderos que se bifurcan* (Sur, Buenos Aires, 1941) in which the tale first appeared? Only ten years ago, it was a mark of arcane erudition and a wink to the initiate to realize that H. Bustos Domecq was the joint pseudonym of Borges and his close collaborator, Adolfo Bioy Casares, or that the Borges who, with Delia In-

22

genieros, published a learned monograph on ancient Germanic and Anglo-Saxon literatures (Mexico, 1951) was indeed the Master. Such information was close-guarded, parsimoniously dispensed, often nearly impossible to come by, as were Borges' poems, stories, essays themselves, scattered, out of print, pseudonymous. I recall an early connoisseur, in the cavernous rear of a bookstore in Lisbon, showing me—this, remember, was in the early 1950's—Borges' translation of Virginia Woolf's *Orlando*, his preface to a Buenos Aires edition of Kafka's *Metamorphosis*, his key essay on the artificial language devised by Bishop John Wilkins, published in *La Nación* on February 8, 1942, and, rarest of rare items, *Dimensions of My Hope*, a collection of short essays issued in 1926 but, by Borges' own wish, not reprinted since. These slim objects were displayed to me with an air of fastidious condescension. And rightly so. I had arrived late at the secret place.

The turning point came in 1961. Together with Beckett, Borges was awarded the Formentor Prize. A year later, *Labyrinths* and *Fictions* appeared in English. Honors rained. The Italian government made Borges *Commendatore*. At the suggestion of M. Malraux, President de Gaulle conferred on his illustrious fellow writer and master of myths the title of Commander of the *Ordre des Lettres et des Arts*. The sudden lion found himself lecturing in Madrid, Paris, Geneva, London, Oxford, Edinburgh, Harvard, Texas. "At a ripe old age," muses Borges, "I began to find that many people were interested in my work all over the world. It seems strange: many of my writings have been done into English, into Swedish, into French, into Italian, into German, into Portuguese, into some of the Slav languages, into Danish. And always this comes as a great surprise to me, because I remember I published a book—that must have been way back in 1932, I think—and at the end of the year I found out that no less than thirty-seven copies had been sold!" A leanness that had its compensations: "Those people are real, I mean every one

23

of them has a face of his own, a family, he lives in his own particular street. Why, if you sell, say, two thousand copies, it is the same thing as if you had sold nothing at all, because two thousand is too vast, I mean for the imagination to grasp . . . perhaps seventeen would have been better or even seven." Cognoscenti will spot the symbolic role of each of these numbers, and of the kabbalistic diminishing series, in Borges' fables.

Today, the secret thirty-seven have become an industry. Critical commentaries on Borges, interviews with, memoirs about, special issues of quarterlies devoted to, editions of, pullulate. Already the 520-page exegetic, biographical, and bibliographical Borges compendium issued in Paris, by *L'Herne*, in 1964, is out of date. The air is gray with theses: on "Borges and Beowulf," on "The Influence of the Western on the Narrative Pace of the Later Borges," on "Borges' Enigmatic Concern with *West Side Story*" ("I have seen it many times"), on "The Real Origins of the Words *Tlön* and *Uqbar* in Borges' Stories," on "Borges and the Zohar." There have been Borges weekends at Austin, seminars at Harvard, a large-scale symposium at the University of Oklahoma—a festivity perhaps previewed in Kafka's *Amerika*. Borges himself was present, watching the learned sanctification of his other self, or, as he calls it, *Borges y yo*. A journal of Borgesian studies is being founded. Its first issue will deal with the function of the mirror and the labyrinth in Borges' art, and with the dreamtigers that wait behind the mirror or, rather, in its silent crystal maze.

With the academic circus have come the mimes. Borges' manner is being widely aped. There are magic turns which many writers, and even undergraduates gifted with a knowing ear, can simulate: the self-deprecatory deflection of Borges' tone, the occult fantastications of literary, historical reference which pepper his narrative, the alternance of direct, bone-spare statement with sinuous evasion. The key images and heraldic markers of the Borges world have

passed into literary currency. "I've grown weary of labyrinths and mirrors and of tigers and of all that sort of thing.
Especially when others are using them. . . . That's the
advantage of imitators. They cure one of one's literary ills.
Because one thinks: there are so many people doing that
sort of thing now, there's no need for one to do it any more.
Now let the others do it, and good riddance." But it is not
pseudo-Borges that matters.

The enigma is this: that tactics of feeling so specialized,
so intricately enmeshed with a sensibility that is private in
the extreme, should have so wide, so natural, an echo. Like
Lewis Carroll, Borges has made of his autistic dreams
discreet but exacting summons which readers the world
over are responding to with a sense of recognition. Our
streets and gardens, the arrowing of a lizard across the
warm light, our libraries and circular staircases are beginning to look precisely as Borges dreamed them, though the
sources of his vision remain irreducibly singular, hermetic,
at moments almost moon-mad.

The process whereby a fantastically private picture of
the world leaps beyond the wall of mirrors behind which
it was created, and reaches out to change the general landscape of awareness, is manifest but exceedingly difficult to
talk about (how much of the vast critical literature on
Kafka is baffled verbiage). That Borges' entrance on the
larger scene of the imagination was preceded by a local
genius of extreme rigor and linguistic *métier* is certain. But
that will not get us very far. The fact is that even lame
translations communicate much of his spell. The message,
set in a kabbalistic code, written, as it were, in invisible
ink, thrust, with the proud casualness of deep modesty,
into the most fragile of bottles, has crossed the seven seas
(there are, of course, many more in the Borges atlas, but
they are always multiples of seven), to reach every kind
of shore. Even to those who know nothing of his masters
and early companions—Lugones, Macedonio Fernandez,
Evaristo Carriego—or to whom the Palermo district of

Buenos Aires and the tradition of gaucho ballads are little more than names, have found access to Borges' *Fictions*. There is a sense in which the Director of the Biblioteca Nacional of Argentina is now the most original of Anglo-American writers. This extraterritoriality may be a clue.

Borges is a universalist. In part, this is a question of upbringing, of the years from 1914 to 1921, which he spent in Switzerland, Italy, Spain. And it arises from Borges' prodigious talents as a linguist. He is at home in English, French, German, Italian, Portuguese, Anglo-Saxon, and Old Norse, as well as in a Spanish that is constantly shot through with Argentine elements. Like other writers whose sight has failed, Borges moves with a cat's assurance through the sound-world of many tongues. He tells memorably of "Beginning the Study of Anglo-Saxon Grammar":

> At fifty generations' end
> (And such abysses time affords us all)
> I returned to the further shore of a great river
> That the vikings' dragons did not reach,
> To the harsh and arduous words
> That, with a mouth now turned to dust,
> I used in my Northumbrian, Mercian days
> Before I became a Haslam or a Borges. . . .
> Praised be the infinite
> Mesh of effect and causes
> Which, before it shews me the mirror
> In which I shall see no one or I shall see another,
> Grants me now this contemplation pure
> Of a language of the dawn.

"Before I became a Borges." There is in Borges' penetration of different cultures a secret of literal metamorphosis. In "Deutsches Requiem," the narrator becomes, *is*, Otto Dietrich zu Linde, condemned Nazi war criminal. Vincent Moon's confession, "The Shape of the Sword," is a classic in the ample literature of the Irish troubles. Elsewhere,

Borges assumes the mask of Dr. Yu Tsun, former professor of English at the *Hochschule* at Tsingtao, or of Averroes, the great Islamic commentator on Aristotle. Each
quick-change brings with it its own persuasive aura, yet
all are Borges. He delights in extending this sense of the
unhoused, of the mysteriously conglomerate, to his own
past: "I may have Jewish ancestors, but I can't tell. My
mother's name is Acevedo: Acevedo may be a name for a
Portuguese Jew, but again it may not. . . . The word
acevedo, of course, means a kind of tree; the word is not
especially Jewish, though many Jews are called Acevedo.
I can't tell." As Borges sees it, other masters may derive
their strength from a similar stance of strangeness: "I
don't know why, but I always feel something Italian, something Jewish about Shakespeare, and perhaps Englishmen
admire him because of that, because it's so unlike them."
It is not the specific doubt or fantastication that counts. It
is the central notion of the writer as a guest, as a human
being whose job it is to stay vulnerable to manifold strange
presences, who must keep the doors of his momentary
lodging open to all winds:

> I know little—or nothing—of my own forebears;
> The Borges back in Portugal; vague folk
> That in my flesh, obscurely, still evoke
> Their customs, and their firmnesses and fears.
> As slight as if they'd never lived in the sun
> And free from any trafficking with art,
> They form an indecipherable part
> Of time, of earth, and of oblivion.

This universality and disdain of anchor is directly reflected in Borges' fabled erudition. Whether or not it is
"merely put there as a kind of private joke," the fabric of
bibliographical allusions, philosophic tags, literary cita-
tions, kabbalistic references, mathematical and philologi-
cal acrostics which crowd Borges' stories and poems is,
obviously, crucial to the way he experiences reality. A per-

ceptive French critic has argued that in an age of deepening illiteracy, when even the educated have only a smattering of classical or theological knowledge, erudition is of itself a kind of fantasy, a surrealistic construct. Moving, with muted omniscience, from eleventh-century heretical fragments to baroque algebra and multi-tomed Victorian *œuvres* on the fauna of the Aral Sea, Borges builds an antiworld, a perfectly coherent space in which his mind can conjure at will. The fact that a good deal of the alleged source material and mosaic of allusion is a pure fabrication—a device which Borges shares with Nabokov and for which both may be indebted to Flaubert's *Bouvard et Pécuchet* —paradoxically strengthens the impression of solidity. Pierre Menard stands before us, instantaneously substantial and implausible, through the invented catalogue of his "visible works"; in turn, each arcane item in the catalogue points to the meaning of the parable. And who would doubt the veracity of the "Three Versions of Judas" once Borges has assured us that Nils Runeberg—note the runes in the name—published *Den hemlige Frälsaren* in 1909 but did not know a book by Euclides da Cunha (*Revolt in the Backlands*, exclaims the reader) in which it is affirmed that for the "heresiarch of Canudos, Antonio Conselheiro, virtue 'was almost an impiety' "?

Unquestionably, there is humor in this polymath montage. And there is, as in Pound, a deliberate enterprise of total recall, a graphic inventory of classical and Western civilization in a time in which much of the latter is forgot or vulgarized. Borges is a curator at heart, a treasurer of unconsidered trifles, an indexer of the antique truths and waste conjectures which throng the attic of history. All this arch learning has its comical and gently histrionic sides. But a much deeper meaning as well.

Borges holds, or, rather, makes precise imaginative use of, a kabbalistic image of the world, a master metaphor of existence, which he may have become familiar with as early as 1914, in Geneva, when reading Gustav Meyrink's novel *The Golem*, and when in close contact with the scholar Maurice Abramowicz. The metaphor goes something like this: the Universe is a great Book; each material and mental phenomenon in it carries meaning. The world is an immense alphabet. Physical reality, the facts of history, whatever men have created, are, as it were, syllables of a perpetual message. We are surrounded by a limitless network of significance, whose every thread carries a pulse of being and connects, ultimately, to what Borges, in an enigmatic tale of great power, calls the Aleph. The narrator sees this inexpressible pivot of the cosmos in the dusty corner of the cellar of the house of Carlos Argentino in Garay Street on an October afternoon. It is the space of all spaces, the kabbalistic sphere whose center is everywhere and whose circumference is nowhere, it is the wheel of Ezekiel's vision but also the quiet small bird of Sufi mysticism, which, in some manner, contains all birds: "I was dizzy and I wept, for mine eyes had beheld this secret and conjectural object, whose name is usurped by men, but which no man has looked upon: the inconceivable universe."

From the point of view of the writer, "the universe, which others call the Library," has several notable features. It embraces *all* books, not only those that have already been written, but every page of every tome that will be written in the future and, which matters more, that could conceivably be written. Re-grouped, the letters of all known or lost scripts and alphabets, as they have been set down in extant volumes, can produce every imaginable human thought, every line of verse or prose paragraph to the limits of time. The Library also contains all extant languages and those languages that either have perished or are yet to come. Plainly, Borges is fascinated by the notion, so prominent in the linguistic speculations of the Kabbala and of Jacob Boehme, that a secret primal speech, an *Ur-sprache* from before Babel, underlies the multitude of human tongues. If, as blind poets can, we pass our fin-

29

gers along the living edge of words—Spanish words, Russian words, Aramaic words, the syllables of a singer in Cathay—we shall feel in them the subtle beat of a great current, pulsing from a common center, the final word made up of all letters and combinations of letters in all tongues that is the name of God.

Thus, Borges' universalism is a deeply felt imaginative strategy, a maneuver to be in touch with the great winds that blow from the heart of things. When he invents fictitious titles, imaginary cross-references, folios and writers that have never existed, Borges is simply re-grouping counters of reality into the shape of other possible worlds. When he moves, by word-play and echo, from language to language, he is turning the kaleidoscope, throwing the light on another patch of the wall. Like Emerson, whom he cites indefatigably, Borges is confident that this vision of a totally meshed, symbolic universe is a jubilation: "From the tireless labyrinth of dreams I returned as if to my home to the harsh prison. I blessed its dampness, I blessed its tiger, I blessed the crevice of light, I blessed my old, suffering body, I blessed the darkness and the stone." To Borges, as to the transcendentalists, no living thing or sound but contains a cipher of all.

This dream-logic—Borges often asks whether we ourselves, our dreams included, are not being dreamed from without—has generated some of the most witty, original short fiction in Western literature. "Pierre Menard," "The Library of Babel," "The Circular Ruins," "The Aleph," "Tlön, Uqbar, Orbis Tertius," "Averroes' Search" are laconic masterpieces. Their concise perfection, as that of a great poem, builds a world that is closed, with the reader inescapably inside it, yet open to the widest resonance. Some of the parables, scarcely a page long, such as "Ragnarök," "Everything and Nothing" or "Borges and I," stand beside Kafka's as the only successes in that notoriously labile form. Had he produced no more than the *Fictions* (1956), Borges would rank among the very few fresh dreamers since Poe and Baudelaire. He has, that being the mark of a truly major artist, deepened the landscape of our memories.

Nonetheless, despite its formal universality and the vertigo breadths of his allusive range, the fabric of Borges' art has severe gaps. Only once, in a story called "Emma Zunz," has Borges realized a credible woman. Throughout the rest of his work, women are the blurred objects of men's fantasies or recollections. Even among men, the lines of imaginative force in a Borges fiction are stringently simplified. The fundamental equation is that of a duel. Pacific encounters are cast in the mode of a collision between the "I" of the narrator and the more or less obtrusive shadow of "the other one." Where a third person turns up, his will be, almost invariably, a presence alluded to or remembered or perceived, unsteadily, at the very edge of the retina. The space of action in which a Borges figure moves is mythical but never social. Where a setting of locale or historical circumstance intrudes, it does so in free-floating bits, exactly as in a dream. Hence the weird, cool emptiness which breathes from many Borges texts as from a sudden window on the night. It is these lacunae, these intense specializations of awareness, which account, I think, for Borges' suspicions of the novel. He reverts frequently to the question. He says that a writer whom dimmed eyesight forces to compose mentally, and, as it were, at one go, must stick to very short narratives. And it is instructive that the first important fictions follow immediately on the grave accident which Borges suffered in December, 1938. He feels also that the novel, like the verse epic before it, is a transitory form: "the novel is a form that may pass, doubtless will pass; but I don't think the story will . . . It's so much older." It is the teller of tales on the highroad, the *skald*, the raconteur of the pampas, men whose blindness is often a statement of the brightness and crowding of life they have experienced, who incarnate Borges' notion of the writer. Homer is often invoked as a

31

talisman. Granted. But it is as likely that the novel represents precisely the main dimensions lacking in Borges. The rounded presence of women, their relations to men, are of the essence of full-scale fiction. As is a matrix of society. Number theory and mathematical logic charm Borges (see his "Avatars of the Tortoise"). There has to be a good deal of engineering, of applied mathematics, in a novel.

The concentrated strangeness of Borges' repertoire makes for a certain preciousness, a rococo elaboration that can be spellbinding but also airless. More than once, the pale lights and ivory forms of his invention move away from the active disarray of life. Borges has declared that he regards English literature, including American, as "by far the richest in the world." He is admirably at home in it. But his personal anthology of English writers is a curious one. The figures who signify most to him, who serve very nearly as alternate masks to his own person, are De Quincey, Robert Louis Stevenson, G. K. Chesterton, and Rudyard Kipling. Undoubtedly, these are masters, but of a tangential kind. Borges is perfectly right to remind us of De Quincey's organ-pealing prose, and of the sheer control and economy of recital in Stevenson and Kipling. Chesterton is a very odd choice, though again one can make out what *The Man Who Was Thursday* has contributed to Borges' love of charade and high intellectual slapstick. But not one of these writers is among the natural springs of energy in the language or in the history of feeling. And when Borges affirms, teasingly perhaps, that Samuel Johnson "was a far more English writer than Shakespeare," one's sense of the willfully bizarre sharpens. Holding himself beautifully aloof from the bombast, the bullying, the strident ideological pretensions that characterize so much of current letters, Borges has built for himself a center that is, as in the mystical sphere of the Zohar, also a far-out place.

He himself seems conscious of the drawbacks. He has said, in more than one recent interview, that he is now aiming at extreme simplicity, at composing short tales of a flat, sinewy directness. The spare encounter of knife against knife has always fascinated Borges. Some of his earliest and best work derives from the legends of knifings in the Palermo quarter of Buenos Aires, and from the heroic razzias of gauchos and frontier soldiers. He takes eloquent pride in his warring forebears: in his grandfather, Colonel Borges, who fought the Indians and died in a revolution; in Colonel Suarez, his great-grandfather, who led a Peruvian cavalry charge in one of the last great battles against the Spaniards; in a great-uncle who commanded the vanguard of San Martín's army:

> My feet tread the shadows of the lances that spar for the kill. The taunts of my death, the horses, the horsemen, the horses' manes, tighten the ring around me. . . . Now the first blow, the lance's hard steel ripping my chest, and across my throat the intimate knife.

"The Intruder," a very short story, illustrates Borges' present ideal. Two brothers share a young woman. One of them kills her so that their fraternity may again be whole. They now enjoy a new bond: "the obligation to forget her." Borges himself compares this vignette to Kipling's first tales. "The Intruder" is a slight thing, but flawless and strangely moving. It is as if Borges, after his rare voyage through languages, cultures, mythologies, had come home, and found the Aleph in the next patio.

In a wonderful poem, "In Praise of Darkness," which equivocates with amused irony on the fitness of a man nearly blind to know all books but to forget whichever he chooses, Borges numbers the roads that have led him to his secret center:

> These roads were footsteps and echoes,
> women, men, agonies, rebirths,
> days and nights,
> falling asleep and dreams,

each single moment of my yesterdays
and of the world's yesterdays,
the firm sword of the Dane and the moon of the
    Persians,
the deeds of the dead,
shared love, words,
Emerson, and snow, and so many things.
Now I can forget them. I reach my center,
my mirror.
Soon I shall know who I am.

It would be foolish to offer a simple paraphrase for that final core of meaning, for the encounter of perfect identity which takes place at the heart of the mirror. But it is related, vitally, to freedom. In an arch note, Borges has come out in defense of censorship. The true writer uses allusions and metaphors. Censorship compels him to sharpen, to handle more expertly the prime instruments of his trade. There is, implies Borges, no real freedom in the loud graffiti of erotic and political emancipation that currently pass for fiction and poetry. The liberating function of art lies in its singular capacity to "dream against the world," to structure worlds that are *otherwise*. The great writer is both anarchist and architect, his dreams sap and rebuild the botched, provisional landscape of reality. In 1940, Borges called on the "certain ghost" of De Quincey to "Weave nightmare nets / as a bulwark for your island." His own work has woven nightmares in many tongues, but far more often dreams of wit and elegance. All these dreams are, inalienably, Borges'. But it is we who wake from them, increased.

CRY HAVOC

Lecturing at Oxford in 1870, Ruskin stated what was to him and his audience almost a platitude when he said, "Accuracy in proportion to the rightness of the cause, and purity of the emotion, is the possibility of fine art. You cannot paint or sing yourself into being good men; you must be good men before you can either paint or sing, and then the colour and sound will complete in you all that is best." In 1948, in *What Is Literature?*, Sartre made the point more specific, but again with assumptions old as Plato about the essential morality and humanism of art: "No one could suppose for an instant that it would be possible to write a good novel in praise of anti-semitism." In a footnote, Sartre challenges those who would disagree with him to name such a novel. If you counter that such a book *might* be written, he says, you are merely taking refuge in abstract theorizing.

Matters are, however, not so straightforward. Even if we set aside the fact that a work of art or literature can affect its audience in unforeseeable ways, that a particular play or picture may move one man to compassion and another to hatred, there is now a good deal of evidence that artistic sensibility and the production of art are no bar to active barbarism. It is a fact, though one with which neither our theories of education nor our humanistic, liberal ideals have even begun to come to grips, that a human be-

35

ing can play Bach in the evening, and play him well, or read Pushkin, and read him with insight, and proceed in the morning to do his job at Auschwitz and in the police cellars. The assumption of humane culture so serene in Ruskin, Sartre's confident identification of literature and freedom, no longer hold. Perhaps they were naïve; so much great art, literature, music has flourished under tyranny and under the patronage of violence. For the modern instance, we need think only of the politics of Yeats, T. S. Eliot, and Pound to resist any facile congruence between the creation of major poetry and the kind of radical humanism, of libertarian commitment, that Ruskin and Sartre had in mind. And in one case (though, as I shall point out, there is a second and even more perplexing example), the most extreme form of political barbarism has coincided with a body of work that a number of critics set in the forefront of modern literature.

The facts about Louis-Ferdinand Céline are worth recalling if only because of the falsifications, dramatic half truths, and professions of mystery with which his apologists cloud the air. In 1937, Céline published *Bagatelles pour un Massacre*, in which he cried out for the eradication of all Jews from Europe, in which he described the Jews as ordure, as subhuman garbage to be thoroughly disposed of if civilization was to regain its vigor and peace be preserved. If we except certain obscure pamphlets published in eastern Europe at the turn of the century and associated with the forgery of the so-called "Protocols of Zion," Céline's was the first public program for what was to become Hitler's "final solution." A second anti-semitic screed, *L'Ecole des Cadavres*, followed in 1938. *Les Beaux Draps*, published in 1941, set out the author's conviction that the defeat and *misère* of France were the direct result of Jewish intrigue, Jewish foulness, and the well-known pestilence of semitic influence and treason in high places. In 1943, when Jewish men, women, and children were being deported from every corner of western Europe, to be tortured to death and made nameless ash, Louis-Ferdinand Céline republished *Bagatelles pour un Massacre*, with appropriate anti-semitic photographs.

The fact that these texts have not been translated into English and that it is nearly impossible to quote from them without physical revulsion makes it necessary to underline their character. With a scatological crudity comparable only to that of Streicher's *Stürmer*, Céline depicts the Jew as the venomous louse in the body of Western culture. The Jew is shown to be a racial abortion, a nightmarish aggregate of filth and cunning, of sterile intelligence and avarice. He must be castrated or totally isolated from the rest of mankind. His influence is everywhere, but many gentiles are unable to detect the reek of marsh gas. Let the Jew henceforth wear a plainly visible emblem of his subhuman status. In 1937 and 1938, these screaming tracts were like matches set to oil. By 1943, they had become an accompaniment—obscene, mocking, and triumphant—to daily atrocity. After the Allied landings, Céline joined various dignitaries and hooligans of the French pro-Nazi establishment at Siegmaringen, in Germany. In March of 1945, Céline, furnished with a German safe-conduct, succeeded in making his way to Denmark. Imprisoned in Copenhagen between December of 1945 and June of 1947, he benefited by an amnesty and returned to France in June of 1951. He died ten years later, almost alone and generally despised.

Since then, however, critics have gone back to Céline's work and a strong case has been put not only for its intrinsic merit but for the decisive influence it has had on modern fiction. Increasingly, it does look as if the novels of Günter Grass, of William Burroughs, and of Norman Mailer would not have been written without Céline's precedent. Allen Ginsberg expresses a whole trend of opinion when he terms Céline's *Journey to the End of Night* "the first genius international beat XX century picaresque novel written in modern classical personal comedy prose by the funniest & most intelligent of mad Doctors whose least tenderness is an immortal moment." In France, Céline's novels are appearing in the Pléiade edition—an outward consecration of classic status—and they have recently been reissued in, or newly translated into, English. A writer who proclaimed the Jew to be excrement and democracy a foul joke is now the object of a considerable critical and academic cult. In paperback, *Journey to the End of Night* figures prominently on the university-bookstore shelf. Obviously, there is a puzzle here, and one that may have bearing beyond the particular case. What light can the work of Céline throw on the nature of imaginative creation, on the vexed problem of the humaneness or amoralism of art and literature? Does Céline offer a genuine counterexample to Sartre's hopeful claim?

One approaches *Céline and His Vision* (New York University Press, 1968) with high expectations. Dr. Erika Ostrovsky is known for her assiduity in studying Céline's voluminous manuscripts, for her determination to clarify obscure points in Céline's career and bibliography. She has plunged heart and soul into her subject, and it is owing to her work and that of Professor Michel Beaujour that New York University is now a center for Céliniana of every kind. Unfortunately, Dr. Ostrovsky has come close to producing that all too frequent sort of academic criticism, the non-book. What we find is a long string of quotations from Céline's novels, interrupted by quotations from other critics of admirers of Céline and tied together by comments from Dr. Ostrovsky in a monotone of portentous ecstasy. The argument of the book can fairly be summed up in a single set of antinomies: Céline's world is "a jail, a trap, a disgrace, a sewer" and "the odor of putrefaction hangs over everything"; nevertheless, the "purging by pity and terror takes place," and on the far side of Céline's vision of madness and excrement there lies the redemptive sphere of "fantasy, poetry, and myth." This perfectly reasonable though by no means original proposition is underscored by constant apocalyptic flourishes:

38

It is as impossible for Céline to give us the re-
deeming side of the picture as it would be for an
avenging angel to wander through a sunny and fruitful countryside, or for the apocalyptic beast not to
graze in regions of a starker nature. Neither can walk
lightly; their relentless tread brings waste and dev-
astation to the earth. Even before their dread figures
appear on the horizon, one can feel the trembling of
the ground and hear the ominous call which summons them. Its sound is heard here and there in all
the works of Céline, sometimes as faint as the notes
of a horn or disguised as a grotesque, humorous discord, sometimes resounding in all its threatening
diapason.

The true perplexities of the case are skimped, and in the
crucial matter of Céline's racism and its murderous implications Dr. Ostrovsky's treatment verges on the frivolous.
What is one to make of her notation that *Bagatelles pour
un Massacre* "brought on accusations of anti-semitism, pro-
Nazi sentiment, and even collaboration"? Or of the diffidence of the statement that "one cannot help but be struck
by the admittedly objectionable point of view expressed in
these pamphlets" (has Dr. Ostrovsky tried to wade through
this long, nauseating book)? Dr. Ostrovsky allows that
these are "undoubtedly dangerous, if not downright lethal
utterances" and does say, though in a footnote, that Céline
expressed no outrage when the Nazis began carrying out
his hideous fantasies. But "the reasons underlying the writing of these works are far from clear and would demand
much careful and impartial research before they could be
elucidated with some objectivity." The question of Céline's
famous and reiterated calls to mass murder—for that is exactly what *Bagatelles* leads to—"is not within the scope of
this study."

There is no joy in rejecting a book by an industrious
young scholar, especially a first book. But these sentences

point to that dissociation between professional zeal and true accuracy of spirit, between the humanities and the humane, that marks so much of present academic work in literature. In the context in which they are offered, "impartial research," "elucidated with some objectivity," and "not within the scope" seem painful evasions of the issue in hand. To say that "Céline disparagingly refers to Jews and Germans in his various writings" without immediately drawing the vital distinction between the two intensities of reference, without telling the reader that *boches* carries a charge of dismissive loathing entirely different from *youtres*, is to interpose a screen before the real complications and indecencies of the case. Elsewhere, Dr. Ostrovsky is all passion and commitment. There is nothing "impartial" or "objective," nor ought there to be, about her encomium of Céline's "genius." She invokes Pascal, Goya, Dostoevski for comparison. But at the heart of the problem there is a vacuum, and the suggestion of a bow to academic decorum. It is to the novels and tracts themselves that we must go back if we hope to see Céline whole—a return complicated, as Dr. Ostrovsky rightly points out, by the fact that Céline's postwar fiction is difficult to obtain and by the more obvious fact that most of his political writings were pulped after the liberation of France. Ralph Manheim's virtuoso translation of *Death on the Installment Plan* is a great help. What is required now is more readily available editions and translations of *D'un Château l'Autre* and *Nord*, which recount Céline's journeying through the vulgar hell of the German collapse.

There are obviously different approaches to the problems posed by Céline's work and great influence. There is a medical reading, whereby the grave head wound suffered by Céline in 1914 gradually affected his reason and engendered the insane hatreds and scatological obsessions of his later writings. One may argue that Céline's vision of the waste and horror of war made his intimations of a second World War a maddening torture. To avoid that catastrophe, to arrive at an understanding with Germany at what-

ever price, was the supreme duty of an honest man. So far
as the Jews were an obstacle to this understanding, so far
as their very presence in Europe caused psychological ten-
sion and kindled ultra-nationalist sentiments, they must be
eliminated. In Céline, a justifiable pacifism went mad.
Metaphorically, it can be argued that his loathing of the
human animal—his view of the world as "a mixture of
asylum and slaughterhouse," in Dr. Ostrovsky's phrase—
induced a specific detestation of the Jews. There is in the
Jewish presence a kind of flagrant, ostentatious humanity,
a resilient at-homeness in the world. When carried to ex-
tremes, misanthropy will soon find the Jew in its path.

Undoubtedly, Céline's infernal sociology had deep roots
in his sense of the French language. He used that language
with both a sweep and an idiomatic intensity equaled perhaps only by Rabelais and Diderot, from both of whom he
learned much. The style that made *Journey to the End of
Night* an event in the history of modern prose is a deafen-
ing, nerve-rending barrage, a breathless accumulation of
invective, scabrous direct address, slang, and colloquial
idiom tied together—or, rather, put into a loud, fiercely
evocative Morse code—by Céline's famous use of dots and
dashes instead of regular punctuation. Céline handled the
French language like an earthmover, digging deep into its
argotic traditions, into the raw speech of Parisian slums
and hospital wards, into the visceral tonalities of patois,
and lifting to the light a trove of words, popular elisions,
technical exactitudes left out of view in the habitual decorum and shapeliness of the French literary idiom. Céline
restored to the novel what it lacked in the hands of Gide
and Proust, what it had possessed in Zola—a frank physi-
cality. Fine as it is, Ralph Manheim's rendering of the
brawl between father and son in *Death on the Installment
Plan* gives only a partial reflection of the sickening power
of the original:

> I'm caught up in the dance . . . I stumble, I
> fall . . . That does it, I've got to finish the stink-

41

ing bastard! Bzing! He's down again . . . I'm
going to smash his kisser! . . . So he can't talk any-
more . . . I'm going to smash his whole face . . .
I punch him on the ground . . . He bellows . . .
He gurgles . . . That'll do. I dig into the fat on his
neck . . . I'm on my knees on top of him . . . I'm
tangled up in his bandages . . . both my hands are
caught. I pull. I squeeze. He's still groaning . . .
He's wriggling . . . I weigh down on him . . .
He's disgusting . . . He squawks . . . I pound
him . . . I massacre him . . . I'm squatting down
. . . I dig into the meat . . . It's soft . . . He's
drooling . . . I tug . . . I pull off a big chunk of
mustache . . . He bites me, the stinker! . . . I
gouge into the holes . . . I'm sticky all over . . .
my hands skid . . . he heaves . . . he slips out of
my grip. He grabs me around the neck. He squeezes
my windpipe . . . I squeeze some more. I knock
his head against the tiles . . . He goes limp . . .
He's soft under my legs . . . He sucks my thumb
. . . he stops sucking . . . Phooey! I raise my
head for a minute . . . I see my mother's face on a
level with mine. . . .

Céline's identification with the historical and local genius
of the French tongue was so much the core of his deranged
being that he must have hated the unhoused, esperanto
trait in the Jewish sensibility. As his tracts make plain, he
could not accept the literary mastery of French achieved by
such "outsiders" as Proust, Henry Bernstein, and Maurois,
wanderers at home in several languages but earthbound in
none.

What is absolutely certain is the unity of Céline's world
image (he wrote the childishly anti-semitic play *L'Eglise*
at the same time as or even earlier than his first novel).
To separate the novels from the prophetic and inflamma-
tory pamphlets is not only dishonest; it is to relinquish any

chance of coherent insight into this single and singular personage. The frenetic energy, the populist oratory, the Rabelaisian genius for magnification that animate the *Journey* and *Death on the Installment Plan* are equally overwhelming in *Bagatelles* and *L'Ecole des Cadavres*. Whole pages, memorable in their hysterical élan, are interchangeable between the fictions and the libels. Nor did Céline recant. Dr. Ostrovsky's statement that he refuted the charges made against him at the time of his condemnation is at best ingenuous. What he sought to refute were allegations—some true, others false—regarding active collaboration with the occupiers. The man was of a piece, and here again the specific quality of his great gift affords a lead.

One of the ways of thinking responsibly about Céline is to ask whether or in what degree words had become a substitute for reality. Logorrhea is the very condition of Céline's achievement and limitation (his head injury may be pertinent). He was a great master of words but was also mastered by them. Dr. Ostrovsky's study of the manuscripts suggests that close labor lies behind the avalanche of Céline's writings. But it is clear that he had the facility needed to pour out language in fantastic amounts, that each snarl, cry, bout of laughter leads to the next with an inevitable, self-generating rush. If Céline's novels have no natural end, this is not only because of their autobiographical nature—a point in which he clearly resembles Thomas Wolfe—but because the torrent of speech has an autonomous dynamism, a weird inner life stronger, one suspects, than anything else in Céline's bruised, isolated, one might almost say "autistic" consciousness. It is conceivable that Céline, especially after the partial loss of creative confidence that seems to have followed on his return from the Soviet Union in 1936, began taking words for reality, that he no longer related the turbulent geyser of language inside him to any substantive realization. When the facts caught up with his barbarous fancies, when he allowed these fancies to be republished in macabre justification of the facts, Céline was no longer able to tell the one from the other.

It is worth observing that in Céline's true heirs—in Grass, Burroughs, Kerouac—something of the same frantic loquacity prevails. Often their language is animate with energies that exceed the novelty or intelligence of what is being said. The contrasting branch of modernity that leads from Joyce and Proust to Nabokov and Borges is radical in its valuation of time and man but conservative in the formality and tight governance of its expressive means. Céline's letters during the war and after (of which a fair selection appears in the two remarkable Céline issues—3 and 5—of the Paris magazine *L'Herne*) belie any easy notion of mental decline or lapse of control. Even casual notes bear the mark of that gross, fierce rhetoric. But some concept of essential abstraction, of a break between word and fulfillment, may help one approach the undeniable unity of Céline's work and may give a clue to the coexistence of a literary talent of the first rank with obvious moral bestiality.

Though Sartre's statement is overconfident, it does remain true that such coexistence is rare, or at least is rare in cases we can document; the career of Gesualdo suggests that musical genius and an exquisite insight into poetry are not necessarily impediments to repeated murder. What is not clear is whether Céline offers a valid exception to Sartre's proposition. Even at their best, in *Journey* and in such parts of *Death on the Installment Plan* as the narrator's hilarious, lyric, lunatic visit to England, Céline's vision and techniques of presentation border on the pathological. Even in these virtuoso flights, as in certain writings of Swift, the excremental and sadistic compulsion seems to go beyond artistic purpose. It may be that Céline is one of those exceedingly rare cases in which an image of life that can scarcely withstand a moment's adult investigation has by sheer force of words been given the stability, the impact of true literature. The works remain a wild artifice, luminous but unnatural—as are flashes of total vision in the epileptic. Far more disturbing, far more subversive of Ruskin's and Sartre's humanism, would be the case of a man in whom explicit barbarism coexisted with the creation of a classical, imaginatively ordered work of art.

There is such a case. One of the young Fascists of the 1930's on whom Céline exercised great influence was Lucien Rebatet. During the Occupation, M. Rebatet collaborated actively with the Nazis. His denunciations of Resistance fighters in the notorious periodical *Je Suis Partout*, the joy he voiced at the death of Jews and hostages, made Rebatet's name one of the most loathed in France. Arrested at the time of the Liberation, he was sentenced to death. In solitary confinement, with chains on his feet and in daily expectation of the end, he managed to write a vast novel and smuggled more than a thousand pages and fragments of manuscript out of prison. *Les Deux Etendards* was published, in two volumes, by Gallimard in 1951 (a decision reportedly taken on the advice of Camus). The book has been published in German but not in English. It is, in my opinion, a greater work than any of Céline's, with the possible exception of *Journey*, and one of the secret masterpieces of modern literature. It narrates the coming of age, deep amity, and final separation of two young men in France between the wars. They are in love with the same young woman, who is a creation comparable in fullness of life, in physical and psychological radiance, to Tolstoy's Natasha. The articulation of this threefold relationship and the great fugue of erotic fulfillment with which the novel draws to its close are major acts of the imagination. Unlike Céline's fiction, Rebatet's novel has the impersonal authority, the sheer formal beauty of classic art. Pardoned by special decree, Rebatet now lives in Paris in semi-clandestinity. His name remains strictly taboo except among a growing number of readers, many of them young people, to whom *Les Deux Etendards* is a revelation.

Thus, Lucien Rebatet, more than Louis-Ferdinand

Céline, constitutes what theologians call a "mystery." In him a profoundly generous imagination, a grasp of the sanctity of individual life that has led to the invention of lasting literary characters coexist with Fascist doctrines and aims of murderous action openly avowed (Rebatet looks with scorn on any attempts to divide Céline the novelist from Céline the publicist, and on any effort to relegate Céline's or his own convictions to scholarly obscurity). Here we touch genuinely on the puzzle of the dissociation between poetic humanism on the one hand and political sadism on the other, or, rather, on their association in a single psyche. The ability to play and love Bach can be conjoined in the same human spirit with the will to exterminate a ghetto or napalm a village. No ready solution to this mystery and to the fundamental questions it poses for our civilization lies at hand. But recent history has thrust it upon us, and those who regard it as "outside their scope" will hardly bring the study of literature back into touch with the darkened fabric of our lives.

A DEATH OF KINGS

There are three intellectual pursuits, and, so far as I am aware, only three, in which human beings have performed major feats before the age of puberty. They are music, mathematics, and chess. Mozart wrote music of undoubted competence and charm before he was eight. At the age of three, Karl Friedrich Gauss reportedly performed numerical computations of some intricacy; he proved himself a prodigiously rapid but also a fairly deep arithmetician before he was ten. In his twelfth year, Paul Morphy routed all comers in New Orleans—no small feat in a city that, a hundred years ago, counted several formidable chess players. Are we dealing here with some kind of elaborate imitative reflexes, with achievements conceivably in reach of automata? Or do these wondrous miniature beings actually create? Rossini's Six Sonatas for Two Violins, Cello, and Double Bass, composed by the boy during the summer of 1804, are patently influenced by Haydn and Vivaldi, but the main melodic lines are Rossini's, and beautifully inventive. Aged twelve, Pascal seems in fact to have re-created for and by himself the essential axioms and initial propositions of Euclidean geometry. The earliest recorded games of Capablanca and Alekhine contain significant ideas and show marks of personal style. No theory of Pavlovian reflex or simian mimesis will account for the facts. In these three domains we find creation, not

47

infrequently characteristic and memorable, at a fantastically early age.

Is there an explanation? One looks for some genuine relationship between the three activities; in what way do music, mathematics, and chess resemble one another? This is the sort of question to which there ought to be a trenchant —indeed, a classic—reply. (The notion that there *is* a deep affinity is not novel.) But one finds little except shadowy hints and metaphor. The psychology of musical invention, as distinct from mere virtuosity of performance, is all but nonexistent. Despite fascinating hints by the mathematicians Henri Poincaré and Jacques Hadamard, scarcely anything is known about the intuitive and ratiocinative processes that underlie mathematical discovery. Dr. Fred Reinfeld and Mr. Gerald Abrahams have written interestingly on "the chess mind," but without establishing whether there is such a thing and, if there is, what constitutes its bizarre powers. In each of these areas, "psychology" turns out to be principally a matter of anecdotes, among them the dazzling executive and creative showings of child prodigies.

Reflecting, one is struck by two points. It looks very much as if the formidable mental energies and capacities for purposeful combination exhibited by the child master in music, mathematics, and chess are almost wholly isolated, as if they explode to ripeness apart from, and in no necessary relation to, normally maturing cerebral and physical traits. A musical prodigy, an infant composer or conductor, may in every other respect be a small child, petulant and ignorant as are ordinary children of his age. There is no evidence to suggest that Gauss's behavior when he was a young boy, his fluency or emotional coherence, in any way exceeded that of other little boys; he was an adult, and more than a normal adult, solely in respect of numerical and geometric insights. Anyone who has played at chess with a very young and highly gifted boy will have noticed the glaring, nearly scandalous disparity between the ruses

48

and analytic sophistication of the child's moves on the board and his puerile behavior the moment the pieces are put away. I have seen a six-year-old handle a French Defense with tenacious artistry and collapse a moment after the game was ended into a loud, randomly destructive brat. In short, whatever happens in the brain and nervous synapses of a young Mendelssohn, of a Galois, of Bobby Fischer, that otherwise erratic schoolboy, seems to happen in essential separateness. Now, although the latest neurological theories are again invoking the possibility of specialized location—the idea, familiar to eighteenth-century phrenology, that our brains have different areas for different skills or potentials—we simply do not have the facts. Certain very obvious sensory centers exist, it is true, yet we just do not know how or if the cortex divides its multitudinous tasks. But the image of location is suggestive.

Music, mathematics, and chess are in vital respects dynamic acts of location. Symbolic counters are arranged in significant rows. Solutions, be they of a discord, of an algebraic equation, or of a positional impasse, are achieved by a re-grouping, by a sequential reordering of individual units and unit-clusters (notes, integers, rooks or pawns). The child master, like his adult counterpart, is able to visualize in an instantaneous yet preternaturally confident way how the thing should look several moves hence. He sees the logical, the necessary harmonic and melodic argument as it arises out of an initial key relation or the preliminary fragments of a theme. He knows the order, the appropriate dimension, of the sum or geometric figure before he has performed the intervening steps. He announces mate in six because the victorious end position, the maximally efficient configuration of his pieces on the board, lies somehow "out there," in graphic, inexplicably clear sight of his mind. In each instance, the cerebral-nervous mechanism makes a veritable leap forward into a "subsequent space." Very possibly this is a fiercely specialized neurological—one is tempted to say neuro-chemical—ability all but

49

isolated from other mental and physiological capacities and susceptible of fantastically rapid development. Some chance instigation—a tune or harmonic progression picked out on a piano in the next room, a row of figures set out for addition on a shop slate, the sight of the opening moves in a café chess game—triggers a chain reaction in one limited zone of the human psyche. The result is a beauteous monomania.

Music and mathematics are among the pre-eminent wonders of the race. Lévi-Strauss sees in the invention of melody "a key to the supreme mystery" of man—a clue, could we but follow it, to the singular structure and genius of the species. The power of mathematics to devise actions for reasons as subtle, witty, manifold as any offered by sensory experience and to move forward in an endless unfolding of self-creating life is one of the strange, deep marks man leaves on the world. Chess, on the other hand, is a game in which thirty-two bits of ivory, horn, wood, metal, or (in stalags) sawdust stuck together with shoe polish, are pushed around on sixty-four alternately colored squares. To the addict, such a description is blasphemy. The origins of chess are shrouded in mists of controversy, but unquestionably this very ancient, trivial pastime has seemed to many exceptionally intelligent human beings of many races and centuries to constitute a reality, a focus for the emotions, as substantial as, often more substantial than, reality itself. Cards can come to mean the same absolute. But their magnetism is impure. A mania for whist or poker hooks into the obvious, universal magic of money. The financial element in chess, where it exists at all, has always been small or accidental.

To a true chess player, the pushing about of thirty-two counters on 8 x 8 squares is an end in itself, a whole world next to which that of mere biological or political or social life seems messy, stale, and contingent. Even the *patzer*, the wretched amateur who charges out with his knight pawn when the opponent's bishop decamps to R4, feels this daemonic spell. There are siren moments when quite normal creatures otherwise engaged, men such as Lenin and myself, feel like giving up everything—marriage, mortgages, careers, the Russian Revolution—in order to spend their days and nights moving little carved objects up and down a quadrate board. At the sight of a set, even the tawdriest of plastic pocket sets, one's fingers arch and a coldness as in a light sleep steals over one's spine. Not for gain, not for knowledge or renown, but in some autistic enchantment, pure as one of Bach's inverted canons or Euler's formula for polyhedra.

There, surely, lies one of the real connections. For all their wealth of content, for all the sum of history and social institution vested in them, music, mathematics, and chess are resplendently useless (applied mathematics is a higher plumbing, a kind of music for the police band). They are metaphysically trivial, irresponsible. They refuse to relate outward, to take reality for arbiter. This is the source of their witchery. They tell us, as does a kindred but much later process, abstract art, of man's unique capacity to "build against the world," to devise forms that are zany, totally useless, austerely frivolous. Such forms are irresponsible to reality, and therefore inviolate, as is nothing else, to the banal authority of death.

Allegoric associations of death with chess are perennial: in medieval woodcuts, in Renaissance frescoes, in the films of Cocteau and Bergman. Death wins the game, yet in so doing it submits, even if but momentarily, to rules wholly outside its dominion. Lovers play chess to arrest the gnawing pace of time and banish the world. Thus, in Yeats's *Deirdre:*

They knew that there was nothing that could save them,
And so played chess as they had any night
For years, and waited for the stroke of sword.
I never heard a death so out of reach
Of common hearts, a high and comely end.

51

It is this ostracism of common mortality, this immersion of human beings in a closed, crystalline sphere, that the poet or novelist who makes chess his theme must capture. The scandal, the paradox of all-important triviality must be made psychologically credible. Success in the genre is rare. Mr. James Whitfield Ellison's *Master Prim* (1968) is not a good novel, but there are worthwhile points in it. Francis Rafael, the narrator, is sent by his editor to do a cover story on Julian Prim, the rising star in American chess. At first the middle-aged chronicler, established and suburban to the core, and the nineteen-year-old master don't hit it off. Prim is arrogant and abrasive; he has the manners of a sharp-toothed puppy. But Rafael himself once dreamed of becoming a ranking chess player. In the tautest scene in the novel, a series of "pots" games at ten seconds a move between Julian and diverse "pigeons" at the Gotham Chess Club, the novelist and the young killer meet across the board. Rafael almost manages a draw, and there springs up between the two antagonists "a kind of freemasonry of mutual respect." By the last page, Prim has won the United States Chess Championship and is engaged to Rafael's daughter. Mr. Ellison's story has all the elements of a *roman à clef*. Julian's idiosyncrasies and career seem closely based on those of Bobby Fischer, whose personal and professional antagonism toward Samuel Reshevsky—a conflict unusual for its public vehemence even in the necessarily combative world of chess—is the center of the plot. Eugene Berlin, Mr. Ellison's Reshevsky, is the reigning champion. In a game that provides the all too obvious climax, Julian wrests the crown from his hated senior. The game itself, a Queen's Pawn Opening, though very likely based on actual master-play, is of no deep interest or beauty. Berlin's treatment of the defense is unimaginative, and Julian's breakthrough on the twenty-second move hardly merits the excited response provided by the novelist, let alone the Championship. Minor incidents and personalities are also closely modeled on actuality; no aficionado will fail to recognize the Sturdivant brothers or mistake the location of the Gotham Club. What Mr. Ellison does convey is something of the queer, still violence chess engenders. To defeat another human being at chess is to humble him at the very roots of his intelligence; to defeat him easily is to leave him strangely stripped. At a boozy Manhattan soirée, Julian takes on Bryan Pleasant, the English film star, at knight odds and a buck a game. He wins over and over, double or nothing, his "queen appearing and slashing at the enemy like a great enraged beast." In a vindictive display of virtuosity, Julian allows himself less and less time. The naked savagery of his gift suddenly appalls him: "It's like a sickness. . . . It comes over you like a fever and you lose all sense of the way things are. . . . I mean who can you beat in fifteen seconds? Even if you're God. And I'm not God. It's stupid to have to say that, but sometimes I have to say it."

That chess can be to madness close allied is the theme of Stefan Zweig's famous *Schachnovelle* published in 1941 and translated into English as *The Royal Game*. Mirko Czentovic, the World Champion, is aboard a luxurious liner headed for Buenos Aires. For two hundred and fifty dollars a game, he agrees to play against a group of passengers. He beats their combined efforts with contemptuous, maddening ease. Suddenly a mysterious helper joins the browbeaten amateurs. Czentovic is fought to a draw. His rival turns out to be a Viennese doctor whom the Gestapo held in solitary confinement. An old book on chess was the prisoner's sole link with the outside world (a cunning symbolic inversion of the usual role of chess). Dr. B. knows all its hundred and fifty games by heart, replaying them mentally a thousand times over. In the process, he has split his own ego into black and white. Knowing each game so ridiculously well, he has achieved a lunatic speed in mental play. He knows black's riposte even before white has made the next move. The World Champion has condescended to a second round. He is beaten in the first game by the marvel-

ous stranger. Czentovic slows down the rate of play.
Crazed by what seems to him an unbearable tempo and by
a total sense of *déjà vu*, Dr. B. feels the approach of schizophrenia and breaks off in the midst of a further brilliant
game. This macabre fable, in which Zweig communicates
an impression of genuine master-play by suggesting the
shape of each game rather than by spelling out the moves,
points to the schizoid element in chess. Studying openings
and end-games, replaying master games, the chess player
is at once white and black. In actual play, the hand poised
on the other side of the board is in some measure his own.
He is, as it were, inside his opponent's skull, seeing himself
as the enemy of the moment, parrying his own moves and
immediately leaping back into his own skin to seek a
counter to the counterstroke. In a card game, the adver-
sary's cards are hidden; in chess, his pieces are constantly
open before us, inviting us to see things from their side.
Thus there is, literally, in every mate a touch of what is
called "suimate"—a kind of chess problem in which the
solver is required to maneuver his own pieces into mate.
In a serious chess game, between players of comparable
strength, we are defeated and at the same time defeat ourselves. Thus the taste of ash in one's mouth.

The title of Nabokov's early novel *King, Queen, Knave*
refers to a suit of cards. But the primary devices of the
book are based on chess. Mr. Black and Mr. White play
chess as the erotic mock melodrama nears its anticlimax.
Their game precisely mirrors the situation of the characters: "Black's knight was planning to attack White's king
and queen with a forked check." Chess is the underlying
metaphor and symbolic referent throughout Nabokov's
fiction. Pnin plays chess; a chance look at the Soviet chess
magazine *8 × 8* impels the hero of *The Gift* to undertake
his mythical biography of Chernyshevski; the title of *The
Real Life of Sebastian Knight* is a chess allusion, and the
intimation of master-play between two modes of truth runs
through the tale; the duel between Humbert Humbert and

Quilty in *Lolita* is plotted in terms of a chess match whose
stakes are death. These points and the entire role of chess
in Nabokov's opus are set out in Mr. Andrew Field's admirably thorough and perceptive *Nabokov: His Life in Art*
(1967). But Mr. Field rather neglects the masterpiece of
the genre. First written in Russian in 1929, *The Luzhin
Defense* appeared in English in 1964. The whole novel is
concerned with the insubstantial wonders of the game. We
believe in Luzhin's chess genius because Nabokov con-
veys the specialized, freakish quality of his gift. In all other
respects and moves of life, Luzhin is a shambling, infantile
creature, pathetically in search of normal human contact.
When he thinks of the matter at all, human relations seem
to him more or less stylized movements in space; survival
in society depends on one's grasp of more or less arbitrary
rules, less coherent, to be sure, than those which govern a
prise en passant. Personal affliction is an unsolved problem,
as cold and full of traps as are the chess problems composed by the hated Valentinov. Only a poet himself under
the spell of chess could have written the account of the
Luzhin-Turati encounter. Here Nabokov communicates, as
no other writer has done, the secret affinities of chess, music,
mathematics, the sense in which a fine game is a form of
melody and animate geometry:

> Then his fingers groped for and found a bewitch-
> ing, brittle, crystalline combination—which with a
> gentle tinkle disintegrated at Turati's first reply.
> . . . Turati finally decided on this combination—
> and immediately a kind of musical tempest over-
> whelmed the board and Luzhin searched stubbornly
> in it for the tiny, clear note that he needed in order in
> his turn to swell it out into a thunderous harmony.

Absorbed in the game, Luzhin forgets to apply a lit match
to his cigarette. His hand is stung: "The pain immediately
passed, but in the fiery gap he had seen something unbearably awesome, the full horror of the abysmal depths of

55

chess. He glanced at the chessboard and his brain wilted from hitherto unprecedented weariness. But the chessmen were pitiless, they held and absorbed him. There was horror in this, but in this also was the sole harmony, for what else exists in the world besides chess? Fog, the unknown, non-being. . . ."

For what else exists in the world besides chess? An idiotic question, but one that every true chess player has at some time asked himself. And to which the answer is—when reality has contracted to sixty-four squares, when the brain narrows to a luminous blade pointed at a single congeries of lines and occult forces—at least uncertain. There are more possible variants in a game at chess than, it is calculated, there are atoms in this sprawling universe of ours. The number of possible legitimate ways of playing the first four moves on each side comes to 318,979,584,-000. Playing one game a minute and never repeating it, the entire population of the globe would need two hundred and sixteen billion years to exhaust all conceivable ways of playing the first ten moves of Nabokov's Mr. White and Mr. Black. As Luzhin plummets to his death, his carefully analyzed suimate, the chasm of the night and of the chill flagstones below "was seen to divide into dark and pale squares."

So does the world in one's recurrent dream of glory. I see the whole scene before me in mocking clarity. The row of tables at Rossolimo's chess café in Greenwich Village or under the greasy ceiling of a hotel lounge in the town of X (Cincinnati, Innsbruck, Lima). The Grand Master is giving a routine exhibition—thirty-five boards in simultaneous play. The rule on such an occasion is that all his opponents play black and move as soon as he steps to the board. The weaker the play, the more rapid his circuit around the room. The more rapid his wolf's prowl, the more harried and clumsy one's answering moves. I am playing a Sicilian Defense, hanging on, trying to parry that darting hand and the punishing swiftness of its visitations. The Grand Master castles on the fifteenth move and I reply Q-QKt5. Once again his step hastens toward my table, but this time, O miracle, he pauses, bends over the board, and, wonder of celestial wonders, calls for a chair! The hall is unbearably hushed, all eyes are on me. The Master forces an exchange of queens, and there surges up in my memory, with daemonic precision, the vision of the Yates-Lasker game in the seventeenth round of the 1924 World Championship in New York. Black won on that March afternoon. I dare not hope for that; I am not mad. But perhaps once, once in my life, a Master will look up from the board, as Botvinnik looked up at the ten-year-old Boris Spassky during an exhibition game in Leningrad in 1947—look at me not as a nameless *patzer* but as a fellow human being, and say, in a still, small voice, *"Remis."*

THE LANGUAGE ANIMAL

Bees dance exact messages to each other as to the direction, amount, and quality of honey found. Dolphins pipe signals of warning or summons. It may be that the trills and whistles of birds convey rudimentary meaning. Meaning, in fact, is the essence, the underlying structure of natural forms. Colors, sequences, odors, regularities, or salient anomalies of shape and event, all are informant. Almost every phenomenon can be "read" and classed as a statement. It signals danger or solicitation, lack or availability of nourishment; it points toward or away from other significant structures. Living beings, above elementary units, dispose of a large, manifold range of articulation: postures, gestures, colorations, tonalities, secretions, facial mien. Separately or in conjunction, these communicate a message, a unit or unit-cluster of focused information. Life proceeds amid an incessant network of signals. To survive is to receive a sufficient number of such signals, to sort out from the random flux those literally vital to oneself and one's species, and to decode the pertinent signals with sufficient speed and accuracy. An organism failing to do so, either because its receptors are blunted or because it "misreads," will perish. A marmot dies when it misreads—*i.e.*, fails to decode accurately—the message of tint, odor, or texture which differentiates the statement of identity of a venomous mushroom from that of an edible variety. A walker in the city, crossing streets, would not survive if he mistranslated the coded message of red and green—either through some organic deficiency (color-blindness) or because the relevant arbitrary idiom, *red/stop green/go*, had not been taught him or had slipped his memory.

All identity is active statement. It communicates its being to the surrounding world through a set of more or less clear, impressive, and complicated signals. We *are* so far as we can declare ourselves to be, and have full assurance of our asserted existence only when other identities register and reciprocate our life-signals. Signals of elemental individuation: "I am, I am in this place, and of this time." Signals of prime need: "These are my foods, these are the prey I seek in order to live." Signals of defense: "My weapons are this smell, these claws, this spine, these means of camouflage. Approach at your risk." What cannot be communicated, what cannot state its ontological existence and minimal demands, is not alive. "Myself it speaks and spells." It is in the reciprocal nature of the statement of identity, in the need for echo, be it savagely contrary, to confirm one's own being, that lies the root of the Hegelian paradox: the need of one living entity for the presence of another, and the fear and hate engendered by that need.

But, to repeat: the natural modes of information are immensely diverse and susceptible of fantastic refinement. In the message-flight of the bee, the exact angle matters; [1] each beck and volte in the courtship minuet of the moor-hen is an expression of coded meaning; very probably, a pointer can "read" accurately hundreds of gradations of smell.

Comme de longs échos qui de loin se confondent
Dans une ténébreuse et profonde unité,
Vaste comme la nuit et comme la clarté,
Les parfums, les couleurs et les sons se répondent.

Long before man, the planet was many-hued, loud, and odorous with statement and reply. We know of fossils of

---

[1] The standard work on this is, of course, Karl von Frisch's *The Dance Language and Orientation of Bees* (1967).

organic structures three thousand million years old. The development of specific information codes, of signal-systems through which emitter and receiver could formulate and exchange messages of identity, need, and sexual correlation, cannot be much younger. Where there is multi-cellular life, where different phyla coexist and compete, there is, there has to be, the articulation of meaning. Only the inert is mute. Only total death has no statement to make.

I have not until now used the word *language*. An enormous mass of information, of extreme subtlety and specificity, is formulated, transmitted, received, and understood at every point in the life-process. Non-linguistic codes have a far longer history than man. Gesture, bodily stance, the display of certain colors not only precede language but continue to surround and, as it were, infiltrate it at every level (a deaf-mute in mourning garb is making an emphatic and possibly quite complex statement). A world without words can be, and, where organic forms are present, must be, a world full of messages. Language is only one, and probably the most recent, of a great sum of expressive codes. Not only do these other codes persist; they may well outlive language. A post-human planet, so long as zoological phenomena endure, will teem with significant, conventionalized communication, as did the earth in the Paleozoic. After man, there will not be silence.

But the uniqueness of language, the fact that it has existed over what is by geological and biological standards a paltry time-span, the fact that it is only one specialized mechanism of information-storage and conveyance among a host of others, is crucial. It directs us to the decisive recognition that *language* and *man* are correlate, that they imply and necessitate each other.

Other codes used by higher animals may be of remarkable sophistication; in certain regards, such as the memorization and exact decipherment of scent and sound, they may be speedier and more economic than speech. But they are not like language. Language, with its genius and limitations, is unique to man. No other signal-system is at all comparable, or, as Noam Chomsky says, "language appears to be a unique phenomenon, without significant analogue in the animal world." [2] One cannot overstate this fundamental, all-determining point. Not at a time when it is the fashion to describe man as a "naked ape" or a biological species whose main motives of conduct are territorial in the animal sense. The Darwinism of such arguments is more naïve than that of T. H. Huxley, who, toward the close of his life, noted that nothing in the theory of natural selection had accounted for the root fact of human speech. We are, as Hesiod and Xenophon may have been among the first to say, "an animal, a life-form that speaks." Or, as Herder put it, *ein Geschöpf der Sprache*—a "language creature" and, at the same time, a creation of language. Man's "manness," human identity as he can state it to himself and to others, is a speech-function. This is the condition that separates him, by an immense gap, from all other animate beings. Language is his quiddity and determines his pre-eminence. Other species build and war; others develop kinship patterns and have devised the mystery of play. Some, if evidence is right, may even produce rudiments of non-functional art. In blood-chemistry and life-cycle, primates are man's near shadow. But he alone speaks language or, as Chomsky formulates it, does not select "a signal from a finite behavioral repertoire, innate or learned." No view of man's nature which fails to register this essential distinction, which fails to make of our inward and outward linguistic state its starting-point, is adequate to the facts.

I I

The implications are so numerous and far-reaching that we are often hardly aware of them. It requires a fairly

[2] Noam Chomsky, in *Language and Mind* (1968).

strenuous act of extrapolation to see our primarily linguistic dimension, to step momentarily outside our own essential skin.

Man's capacity to articulate a future tense—in itself a metaphysical and logical scandal—his ability and need to "dream forward," to hope, make him unique.[3] Such capacity is inseparable from grammar, from the conventional power of language to exist in advance of that which it designates. Our sense of the past, not as immediately, innately acquired reflexes, but as a shaped selection of remembrance, is again radically linguistic. History, in the human sense, is a language-net cast backward.[4] No animal remembers historically; its temporality is the eternal present tense of the speechless. Our sexuality is shot through with the stimulus and "competing reality" of language. It may well be that our love-making does not differ very much from that of the great apes. But this is to say little. Through its verbalized imaginings, through the rich context of pre-physical and para-physical erotic exchange in which it takes place, human intercourse (a term obviously akin to "discourse") has a profoundly linguistic character.[5] Correlatively, changes of verbal convention, removals or alterations of speech taboos in regard to erotic statement, affect our most intimate, our most immediately physiological sexual conduct. One need only note the correlations between onanism and interior speech or monologue to realize that eros is, in man, a complex idiom, a semantic act involving the entirety of the persona.

If recent structural anthropology is right (and its hypotheses in fact elaborate the suppositions of Leibniz and Herder), those kinship models, those conventions of mu-

---

[3] This notion of the philosophically "scandalous" nature of the future tense is explored by Ernst Bloch in *Das Prinzip Hoffnung* (1959), and his *Tübingener Einleitung in die Philosophie* (1963).

[4] Cf. Thorleif Boman: *Das hebräische Denken im Vergleich mit dem griechischen* (1965).

[5] It is for this reason that such defenders of Sade as Roland Barthes argue that extreme eroticism always represents a linguistic act.

tual identification which underlie all human society, depend vitally on the availability and growth of language. Man's passage from a natural to a cultural state—the single major act in his history—is at every point interwoven with his speech faculties. Incest taboos and the consequent kinship systems that make possible the definition and biosocial survival of a community do not precede language. They most probably evolve with and through it. We cannot prohibit that which we cannot name. Exogamic or endogamic marriage rules can only be formulated and, what is no less important, transmitted where an adequate syntax and verbal taxonomy exist. Language forms quite literally underlie and perpetuate human behavior. The prevalence of promiscuous mating and incest in animals, a prevalence which makes it impossible to speak of "animal cultures" in any but a loosely metaphoric way, is almost certainly a function of the absence of animal languages.[6]

I would go further. Our mechanisms of identity—the enormously intricate procedures of recognition and delimitation which allow me to say that *I am I*, to experience myself, and which, concomitantly, bar me from "experiencing you" except by imaginative projection, by an inferential fiction of similitude—are thoroughly grounded in the fact of language. I suspect that these mechanisms evolved slowly and agonizingly, perhaps over millennia. The recognition of self as against "otherness" is an achievement of formidable difficulty and consequence. The legends of reciprocal denomination which we find all over the earth (Jacob and the Angel, Oedipus and the Sphinx, Roland and Oliver), the motif of mortal combat which ceases only when the antagonists reveal their own names or name each other in an exchange of certified identity, may have in them the shadowy intimation of a long doubt: who am I, who are you, how are we to know that our identities are stable, that we shall not flow into "otherness" as do wind

[6] Cf. Yvan Simonis, *Claude Lévi-Strauss ou la "Passion de l'Inceste"* (1968).

63

and light and water? Even now, identity remains a threatened possession: in the autistic child (so critical a case for
anyone interested in the interdependence of language and
humanity) and in the schizoid, certainty of self has failed
to mature or has broken down.[7] In constant affirmation of
ego, we project on other human beings the silhouette of
our presence. The whole process, statement of self and
response by the "non-self," is dialectic in structure and linguistic in nature. Speech is the systole and diastole of sustained being; it gives inward and outward proof. I establish and preserve my experience of self by a stream of
internalized address. I realize my unconscious, so far as
dreams or the sudden rifts of delirium permit, by listening
for and amplifying "upward" shreds of discourse, of verbal
static, from the dim and middle of the psyche. We do not
speak *to ourselves* so much as *speak ourselves*. We provide
our self-consciousness with its only and constantly renewed
guarantee of particular survival by beaming a current of
words inward. Even when we are outwardly mute, speech
is active within and our skull is like an echo chamber. Correspondingly, we establish the existence of *l'autre*, and our
existence for him, by means of linguistic give and take. All
dialogue is a proffer of mutual cognizance and a strategic
re-definition of self. The Angel names Jacob at the end of
their long match, the Sphinx compels Oedipus to name
himself, to know himself as man. Nothing destroys us more
surely than the silence of another human being. Hence
Lear's insensate fury against Cordelia, or Kafka's insight
that several have survived the song of the Sirens, but none
their silence.

In a sense that cuts much deeper than semantics, our
identity is a first-person pronoun. Monotheism, that transcendental magnification of the image of the human self,
acknowledges this truth when it defines God by a gram-

[7] No one concerned with the philosophy of language can afford to
overlook Dr. Bruno Bettelheim's study of autistic children in *The
Empty Fortress* (1967).

matical tautology: "I am that I am." Neo-Platonism and Gnosticism take the process of linguistic-ontological relationship a step further: "I am the Word, the *Logos* that calls itself and all else into immediate being. I create the world by naming it." Adam is nearest to the divine nature, is most wholly in God's image, when he re-enacts this lexical *poiesis:* "whatsoever Adam called every living creature, that was the name thereof. . . ."

In short, the least inadequate definition we can arrive at of the genus *homo*, the definition that fully distinguishes him from all neighboring life-forms, is this: man is a *zoon phonanta*, a language-animal. And there is no other like him.

III

The "when" and "how" of this uniqueness have been the subject of endless speculation. From Plato to the present, myths and theories about the origins of human speech abound. We seem no nearer to an answer.

> Honesty forces us to admit [writes Chomsky] that we are as far today as Descartes was three centuries ago from understanding just what enables a human to speak in a way that is innovative, free from stimulus control, and also appropriate and coherent. . . . Neither physics nor biology nor psychology gives us any clue as to how to deal with these matters.

It may be that all enquiry into the origins and determinant sub-structure of language has skirted a cardinal dilemma: to inquire into the sources of language by using language (what other instruments have we?) may, necessarily, be a circular process, a juggling with mirrors. Unable, conceptually, to transcend its own linguistic terms of reference, the question begs any conceivable answer. Imagining, as we do, verbally, it may be impossible for us to formulate a condition prior to words. We can, formally, state such a priority, but it will be void of active meaning as is a blind man's notion of color. It may be that the entire image of "linguistic gradualism," of a stage-by-stage advance from pre- or proto-linguistic man to the articulate being we know, is naïve in the extreme. If the concepts of "man" and of "language" are interdependent for their existence, "pre-language man" is a meaningless chimera. Man becomes man as he enters on a linguistic stage. At the outset, in the penumbra of diffuse, threatened identity, speech was probably focused inward; man declared himself only to himself. Verbal exchange, the partial release of the treasure of words into another man's hearing and keeping, may well have come much later. We shall never know. But the question should be seen for what it is: when we ask when or how language began, we are in fact asking "What are the origins of man's humanity"?

Because of this overlap, because any theory of the coming of language is a theory about man's entrance into history, about his passage from an unchanging biological present into the grammar of past, present, and future, recent work in linguistics, genetics, and social anthropology exhibits interesting points of contact. And it might well be that Chomsky overstates the case when he says that neither physics nor biology can give us any clue.

It no longer seems that cranial volume is by itself decisive to man's achievement of humanity. What matters is the development and activation (or development through activation) of electro-chemical hook-ups between as many as possible of the *ca.* one hundred million cells in the brain. Gradations of intensified humanity may be seen as a function of the enlarged use of the cortex. Understood somatically, Nietzsche's imperative *werde was du bist* signifies "harness more and more of your cortex, activate more and more of the total potential of filaments and contact points between neural centers." Presumably, the entire process is one of feed-back: as the needle "finds" and deepens into sound previously imperceptible grooves, so new cerebral requirements engender or trigger new circuits. Life is a coming into being—more or less achieved—of the potential self.

In this self-sustaining dynamism, information is of the essence. Its storage, coding, transmission, and reception are the anatomy of consciousness. (This allows one to say, at a more obvious level, that the larger a man's vocabulary, the more resourceful his syntax, the greater will be his possession of self and the sum of reality on which he can draw.[8]) "Information" is the key term in those models now being used by both molecular biology and linguistics. I realise that the striking analogies of idiom in these two disciplines are, in part, a result of shared metaphor, that they ought not to be over-emphasized. But they are also, in part, cognitive, and one cannot deny the possibility of mutual relevance.[9]

It does appear, on present and manifestly preliminary evidence, as if certain electro-chemical and neuro-chemical processes of mental life might be "semantically" structured. Sensory input, storage, scanning, and subsequent response seem to occur in some kind of syntactical sequence; neither the neuro-chemistry of the human brain nor any human language seems to contain what modern linguists call "structure-independent operations." This may be an important clue. There seems to be, in a sense more than imagistic, a grammar of life-processes, an organic templet from whose sequential organization and genetic activity in man language naturally arises. Language, in turn, reacts on, feeds back to, its physiological matrix. Or, to put it another way, the use of language of itself activates the substratum of linguistic potentiality. More and more synapses, more and more fibers of interrelation are woken into

[8] As early as the 1900's, "self-improvement" courses and nostrums began capitalizing on the insight that "more words will make you a bigger man."

[9] Cf. E. H. Lenneberg, "A Biological Perspective of Language" in New Directions in the Study of Language (1966).

being. In the use of metaphor—a fact of language which Plato recognized as somehow crucial to human excellence—the neuro-physiological and the verbal seem to touch very closely. Metaphor ignites a new arc of perceptive energy. It relates hitherto unrelated areas of experience; such new relation may have a direct organic counterpart as hitherto separate centers of memory and scanning in the cortex are brought "into circuit." [10]

Information, feed-back, coding and de-coding, punctuation so as to ensure the right reading of electro-chemical messages—these are notions shared, at least in part, by molecular biology and generative grammar. The coincidence, in time, of the breakthrough in genetics and of modern structural linguistics from Saussure to Harris and Chomsky does not look accidental.[11] An intimation of life as language, as transmitted information, was in the air. The two currents are congruent. If, as Chomsky proposes, linguistic universals—those orderings which allow us immediately to differentiate what is possible in a language from what is not—"must simply be a biological property of the human mind," then it is likely that the biology of the mind is itself "syntactical." [12] Genetics would be, as some already assert, a special case of information theory. Undoubtedly, the relevant physics and chemistry are of an order of complication beyond our present grasp; and it may well be that our whole concept of what is "physical" and what is "mental" may have to be re-thought and made far subtler than it now is. But, in that future psycho-physiology, the matter of the biological foundations of language will play a decisive role. We may come to understand how, and in what ways, the levels of genetic specificity and sophistication at work in human heredity carry

[10] Cf. E. H. Lenneberg, *Biological Foundations of Language* (1967).
[11] It is Professor Zellig Harris of the University of Pennsylvania who initiates the new linguistics in his *Methods in Structural Linguistics* (1951).
[12] Cf. Noam Chomsky's discussion with Stuart Hampshire (*The Listener*, May 30, 1968).

with them—and are carried by—a unique communicative code. In a manner we cannot as yet formulate with our blunt tools of introspection, it may be that human speech is in some way a counterpart to that decoding and translation of the neuro-chemical idiom which defines and perpetuates our biological existence. The next dimension of psychology, the step that may at last take us beyond a primitive mind/body empiricism, could well be semantic.

A subsidiary, though hardly less difficult, set of questions arises from the fact of the multiplicity of human languages. Why so many? (Three thousand according to some classifications, more than four thousand according to others.) The myth of Babel suggests an early awareness that there is a puzzle here, a curious mystery of waste. But even in Humboldt's great essay *Ueber die Verschiedenheit des Menschlichen Sprachbaues* (1830–35), the question is not posed with sufficient rigor or pressed home.

Why this fantastic diversity of human tongues, making it difficult for communities, often geographically proximate and racially or culturally similar, to communicate? How can such exceeding variety have arisen if, as transformational grammar postulates and biology hints, the underlying grid, the neuro-physiological grooves, are common to all men and, indeed, occasion their humanity? Why, as carriers of the same essential molecular information, do we not speak the same language or a small number of languages corresponding, say, to the small number of genuinely identifiable ethnic types? [13]

No one has come up with a satisfactory hypothesis, and it is a central weakness in generative grammar that Chomsky and his colleagues do not recognize the full scope and importance of the question. How "universal," in fact, are their invariants? And if linguistic universals are a simple, determined biological datum, why the immense

[13] For a recent treatment of this *"particolarismo arcaico"* see Ferruccio Rossi-Landi *"Ideologie della relatività linguistica"* (*Ideologie* 4, 1968).

number and consequent mutual incomprehensibility of local transformations? Natural and evolutionary mechanisms are, in general, economic. The great variety of fauna and flora is by no means inefficient; it represents a naturally selected, maximalized efficiency of adjustment to local need and ecology. We cannot say the same of the world's profusion of mutually incomprehensible tongues. There is a stubborn mystery here, and one that may lead a very long way back.[14]

Evidence suggests that, if anything, the number of different languages was far greater in the past than it is now. Within living memory, scores of ancient and elaborate languages have been snuffed out. There are many South American Indian languages which live, today, only in the recollection, often imperfect, of a handful of informants. The pressures of technological uniformity and the ever increasing premium put on rapid, unambiguous communication are eroding the language atlas. Does this diminution, this evidence of an even greater linguistic proliferation in the past, give a lead? We do not know. One can imagine, but without much cogency, a state in which verbal articulation was almost completely private or esoteric. Each more or less closed knot of human beings, each clan or kinship nucleus on its way to becoming a society, may have had its own speech and guarded the magic of that speech from contamination. We know still of communities which use an ancient idiom internally while sharing a more recent vulgate with their neighbors. We have no facts to go by, and scarcely any hypotheses. But I repeat: no information theory, no model of the growth into being of human consciousness, will be convincing until it accounts for the profoundly startling, "anti-economic" multiplicity of languages spoken on this crowded planet.

[14] I am fully aware that such ethno-linguists as Professor Dell Hymes (see *Language in Culture and Society*, 1964) believe that cultural variety accounts for the immense number and diversity of tongues. But so "anti-economic" a phenomenon does seem to require further explanation and, possibly, an entirely different theoretic model.

IV

Often an intellectual reorientation is identified and seen as a coherent whole only after it has manifested itself locally and in apparently unrelated forms. Looking back now to the years just before the First World War, to the simultaneous developments in linguistics, symbolic logic, and mathematical philosophy, we can recognize the beginnings of a "language revolution." A new theory of meaning and of the central role of the linguistic in man and culture were at work in a wide range of sensibility and formal pursuit.[15] Today, from the vantage point of the synthesis put forward by Lévi-Strauss and Chomsky, or looking back from the shrewd histrionics of John Cage, we can see that very different energies and interests were in fact meshing toward a common impact.

It is in Central Europe, particularly in Vienna and Prague between *ca.* 1900 and 1925, that the "language revolution" took place at the deepest, most consequent level. Like most true revolutions, it had behind it a distinctive failure of nerve. The new linguistics arose from a drastic crisis of language; the mind loses confidence in the act of communication itself. This crisis produced a set of works, closely related in time and place of composition, which are unquestionably among the few classics of our disheveled century. I mean Hofmannsthal's *Lord Chandos Letter*, which, as early as 1902, poses the problem of the deepening gap between language and meaning, between the poet's addiction to personal truth and the eroded mendacities of his idiom; and Hofmannsthal's *Der Schwierige*, in which the protagonist, who has survived live burial in the trenches, finds ordinary chatter and the lofty rhetoric of politics a hideous "indecency." The language-polemics of Karl Kraus, one of the few instances in literature of a

[15] Already in 1903, in *The Principles of Mathematics*, Bertrand Russell wrote: "The study of grammar, in my opinion, is capable of throwing far more light on philosophical questions than is commonly supposed by philosophers."

71

poetry of contempt, belong to this sphere; as does Kraus's maniacal conviction that clarity and purity of syntax are the ultimate test of a society. There is Fritz Mauthner's great work, *Beiträge zu einer Kritik der Sprache*,[16] in which the very survival of language as a conveyor of verifiable meaning and personal responsibility is put in question. Wittgenstein's *Tractatus* and the linguistic-logical exercises of the Vienna Circle are intimately related to the sensibility of Kraus or Mauthner. The latter's notion of the "unspeakable," of that which lies necessarily outside language, closely parallels Wittgenstein's rubric of "the mystical" and the closing proposition of the *Tractatus*.

The same "language crisis" was at work in the arts: in Morgenstern's *Nightsong of the Fish*—a poem of absolute silence, made visible only through prosodic markings over blank, yet somehow extant, "audible" syllables—or in the fictions of Kafka. No writer has ever made of the resistance of language to truth, of the impossibility of adequate human communication, a more honest, a more eloquent statement. Kafka used every word, in a language which he experienced as alien, as if he had purloined it from a secret, dwindling store and had to return it before morning intact. Hermann Broch elaborated Kafka's parables on the temptations of silence. *The Death of Virgil* marks the end of the contract between imagination and reality on which the classic novel was based. In it the poet comes to recognize in the act of poetry, in a commitment to language, a blasphemy against life and the needs of man. One would also want to include in this context the new uses of silence in the music of Schoenberg and Webern, and in particular the "failure of the word" which is the dramatic substance and climax of Schoenberg's *Moses und Aron*.

Obviously, there are forerunners to this extraordinary revaluation of language, to this Central European school

---

[16] The complete text of Mauthner's three-volume treatise appeared in 1923. The wealth and seriousness of its arguments have until now scarcely been followed up.

of silence. If Hölderlin, Rimbaud, and Mallarmé emerge as the begetters of the modern, it is because modernism expressed itself as a questioning of the medium, because it made of its works a constant subversion of the very possibility of stated form. For this tactic, the notorious silences of Hölderlin and Rimbaud and the hermetic sparsities of Mallarmé provided an accredited precedent. But the Vienna-Prague movement had a grimmer quality. It was in the grip of spiritual terror. In these philosophers, poets, and critics was manifest the realization, crystallized by the catastrophe of world war, that humanism, as it had energized European consciousness since the Renaissance, was in a process of collapse. Karl Kraus's premonition of new dark ages, Kafka's eerily exact pre-vision of the holocaust, spring from an acute diagnosis of the breakdown of liberal humanism. In *Auto-da-fé*, Elias Canetti produced the representative fable of a speech-civilization going to violent ruin. Precisely because language had been so central a medium of humane literacy, of the classic legacy of culture, the "language crisis" concentrated a more general devaluation. In the hollowness and death of the word, Mauthner, Wittgenstein, and Broch observed the malady of a whole civilization. (The dominant role of Jews in this movement of terror and genius would be worth assessing. Did the Jew have an especial affinity to the life of language, the written word having been, for so long, his primary homeland?)

Two other contemporaneous directions of thought became implicated in the "language revolution." These were the Moscow (later, Prague) circle of linguistic study, with its strong interest in the poetic and philosophic facets of language; and the practice of logical-semantic analysis we associate with G. E. Moore and Bertrand Russell. Through Russell's misreading of the *Tractatus*—a misreading perhaps strategic, perhaps unavoidable in view of the obsessive guardedness of Wittgenstein's "religiosity" and ultimate ethical purpose—the Vienna-Prague movement and Cam-

73

bridge philosophy overlapped. Wittgenstein's personal career became the symbol of that somewhat unnatural but creative alliance. In turn, via the work and teaching of such "Moscow linguists" as Roman Jakobson, a more technical study of morphology, grammar, and semantics came to influence the general concept of language.[17] (Here again, there is a formidably interesting piece of intellectual history to be written. May one raise the question, for instance, of a possible relationship between homosexuality and certain theories of language as a "game," as a complex of internalized conventions and mirrorings?)

Whatever the variousness and complication of background, the main fact is clear: there occurred in the first quarter of this century a crisis of language and a reexamination of language in the light of that crisis. We are now beginning to be able to judge its range and consequences. I want to touch briefly on three areas of obvious impact: the philosophic, the psychological, and the literary.

V

The idea that all cognition, that the process by which man perceives and relates to the world, is, at bottom, a matter of language is not new. In the eleventh century, Peter Damian gave it pointed expression when he argued that even man's fall into paganism was owing to a flaw of grammar: because heathen speech has a plural for the word "deity," wretched humankind came to conceive of many gods. A similar notion of linguistic totality is implicit in Lenin's query: "History of thought: history of language?" Indeed, one can reasonably divide the history of philosophy between those epistemologies that stress the substantiality, the exterior verifiability and concrete objectification of human experience, and those that emphasize the creative or confining wholeness of their own means of

[17] V. Erlich's *Russian Formalism, History, Doctrine* (1955), and J. Vachek's *The Linguistic School of Prague* (1966) remain the best guides to this development.

statement—*i.e.*, which see man reaching out to reality and inward to himself only so far as language (perhaps his particular language) allows. The distinction is a very rough one precisely because even the most "realistic," the most pragmatically oriented phenomenology will, where it is being honest and severe with itself, remain uneasily aware of its own verbal idiom. No metaphysic is speechless, none escapes from its own vernacular into some realm of pure material evidence.

Much of the lasting vitality of Platonism lies in its subtle realization of this necessary solipsism. Platonism turns on the act of designation, on man's compulsive ability to recognize and map the world according to agreed nomenclature and definition. It focuses on the power of metaphor to reorganize experience by conjoining previously disparate recognitions. The quarrel of Platonism with certain modes of fiction and dramatic mime is a quarrel with a rival, potentially anarchic mapping. Scholasticism, in this respect more Neo-Platonic than Aristotelian, frequently identifies being with statement. The *summa* of words and of accessible reality are one. Each authenticates the other. Hence the literal importance of the image of "the book of life": that book is a lexicon in which names and realities affirm each other's true existence. For Isidore of Seville, etymology is history because the origins of words and that of the objects they articulate are ontologically connected. When mortals speak, they call into being whatever of the world is accessible to their senses and understanding. The exercise of human language enacts, albeit on a microscopically humble scale, the Divine reflex of creation, the *Logos* or "speaking into being" of the universe. Medieval sensibility and the verbal focus of Talmudic and kabbalistic exegesis left their impress on Spinoza. Convinced, as Descartes was,[18] that human controversies and confusions are, in

---

[18] "*Si de verborum significatione inter philosophos semper conveniret fere omnes illorum controversiae tolerentur.*" (Regulae XII, 5.)

"Almost all controversy would cease if there was agreement between philosophers as to the meaning of terms."

essence, a matter of failed communication, of definitions not made or adhered to with sufficient rigor, Spinoza aimed at a grammar of truth. Where we define our terms closely, where we relate these terms in consistent propositions, we shall be able to put questions to which God—or his echoing aggregate which is the World—will give valid reply. One can relate the underlying tone of spirit in Spinoza's *Tractatus* to that of Wittgenstein by glossing the meaning of *"Fall"* (case); where Wittgenstein says *"Die Welt ist alles, was der Fall ist"* (the world is everything that is the case), Spinoza seems to be saying that the world is that which we can take cognisance of only if the syntax, the grammatical "case," of our discourse with it is rightly inflected. (Is there not, I wonder, an even deeper overlap at work here, an awareness that *der Fall* is also "the Fall," that "the case of man" is his fallen condition—a condition whose fatal consequences were Babel and the maddening difficulties we find in seeking to communicate with each other and with reality?)

Two other elements in Spinoza's analytics proved prophetic. These are the pursuit of a mathematical model, the belief that the more it operates like a set of mathematical axioms and demonstrations, the nearer will language be to fulfilling its potential for truth; and the related concept of a genuine *lingua communis*, of a philosophic Esperanto in which all men would—as in algebra—be attaining undoubted conclusions by the use of an agreed, uniquely meaningful code.[19] Both ideas were fruitful. Via Leibniz's work in the calculus and Leibniz's conjectures about a universal idiom perhaps founded on Chinese ideograms, they carry over into the symbolic logic and generative grammars of the twentieth century. Both are attempts to return to Edenic semantics, to that thorough concurrence

[19] See, for example, George Dalgarno's *Ars Signorum* (1661) and Bishop Wilkins' *Essay towards a real character and a philosophical language* (1668) for a proposal of a universal sign language.

between word and object which marked language before the Fall, and before the malediction of mutual incomprehensibility at Babel.

Post-Nietzschean philosophy is largely and self-proclaimedly linguistic. It has, by a deliberate tactic of retrenchment, gathered its strength in what traditional philosophies classified as the vital but only instrumental discipline of logic. Wittgenstein's famous description of philosophic activity as "speech therapy," and his statement "All philosophy is critique of language," cover much of modern ground. The *Principia Mathematica*, Wittgenstein's own *Investigations*, Austin's *Sense and Sensibilia*, the work of Professor Quine, represent a *recul pour mieux sauter*. After the word-epics of nineteenth-century philosophy, after the literal vastness of argument in Hegel, Schopenhauer, and Nietzsche's *Zarathustra*, a good deal of the best in contemporary philosophy embodies a reflex of asceticism, a fastidious severity often mathematical in mien. Thus, symbolic logic and the numbering of propositions in the *Tractatus* instance a comparable search for the clarity and demonstrable coherence of algebraic argument. Here again, Spinoza's *Ethics* may be seen as a distant precedent.

Statements about ourselves and about what is "other" or "outside" the self are, first of all, *statements*. How they are made up, the rules that govern their usage and translation, their incompletions—these are felt to constitute the proper *métier* of philosophy. But that *métier* is itself a matter of statement. Hence the inherently self-conscious, unstable relations of the philosopher and of the philosophical process to the object of his or its activity. Philosophy is meta-language, a kind of discourse about the possibilities and nature of common or, as the case may be, special discourse. Like the diamond-cutter, the philosopher-linguist is a craftsman whose tools are made of the same substance as that which he works on. It is his heuristic job to make this solution explicit, to make us aware of our skin and thus, at least by virtue of momentary mental exercise, able to step outside it while insisting, simultaneously, that we cannot really do so. The best of modern philosophy has something of the penetrating but disembodied incandescence of a beam of light trapped, "imploded," between mirrors.

This, of course, is not the whole story. The common charge brought against linguistic philosophy is, precisely, its reductiveness, its refusal to acknowledge as philosophically relevant such areas as politics, aesthetics, morals, or metaphysics in the old sense. The laser may cut deep, but its focus is absurdly narrow and its insights are, in the last analysis, no better than formal. By demanding criteria of coherence and proof imitative of mathematics and, therefore, quite inapplicable to most patterns of human conduct and aspiration, modern philosophy has abdicated from a consideration of life and has itself become an esoteric game. Chess does not assist mankind in its racked search for transcendent values.

This is obviously a serious accusation. It underlies the estrangement of "pure" from general or "innocently verbalized" philosophy. There is a sense in which both Quine and Sartre are philosophers; but that sense is too diffuse to be of much worth or to induce normal collaboration. To a philosopher-linguist, most of what a Sartre or an Ernst Bloch produces is simply non-sense. The intellectual and social cost of this divorcement is probably high. Nevertheless, the "language revolution" in philosophy has been fiercely educative and will not be undone. The somewhat fatuous naïveté about the nature and limitations of the verbal idiom that led to the style of a Bergson or a Jaspers need not recur. We shall not see again leviathans of print that declare themselves systematic and demonstrative of truth by mere rhetorical fiat. Moreover, even where it excludes traditional moral disputation, even where it questions the truth-function of ethical propositions, a language-therapy such as Wittgenstein's is a distinctly moral act:

by demanding acute self-awareness, by forcing us to put the cards of belief on the table, by making of every perception a scruple and a risk. Valéry's fable of epistemology, *M. Teste*, beautifully renders the relevant asceticism, the thorny elegance which equates a *non sequitur*, a *petitio principii*, or a failure to define one's terms with bad manners.

And though it avoids the grand operatics of theology, linguistic philosophy has made of this exclusion an act of deeply suggestive inference. What lies outside language ought not to be spoken of, cannot be spoken of without gross falsification, but it is by no means negated. As Wittgenstein wrote in 1917: "*Nothing* is lost if one does not seek to say the unsayable. Instead, that which cannot be spoken is—unspeakably—*contained* in that which is said!" [20] This assertion makes the *Tractatus* heir to the anti-rhetoric of Kierkegaard and to Tolstoy's hatred of "style."

By underlining and probing the linguistic anatomy of human consciousness, the language-philosophers have rendered our sense of identity and reach more modest, more vulnerable, but also subtler. Like Monsieur Jourdain, we all know now that we speak prose, and this vulgate condition determines much of our sense of the world. But where such awareness penetrates more traditional and substantive forms of philosophic argument, as, for example, in the writings of Merleau-Ponty, an unmistakable finesse and strength result. A reoccupation of relinquished terrain may lie ahead, a fresh advance from meta-language into language. If it takes place, it will do so in a stoic, highly trained cognizance of the conventionality, of the solipsism of all philosophic statement (of any significant statement *tout court*). The equilibrist will move ahead with his eyes open.

Any model of the rules of the mind leads back to an

[20] Letter to Paul Engelmann, April 9, 1917.

explicit or undeclared psychology. Underneath every logic and epistemology, however prescriptive and neutral they may be, we find a theory of consciousness. It is at the intersections between philosophy and psychology that the new linguistics (or those branches called "psycho-linguistics" and "ethno-linguistics") is proving of great importance. Fundamental to the current approach is a postulate associated with the work of Benjamin Lee Whorf on "language, thought and reality" and, in particular, on the Hopi language-family of the American southwest. It is a postulate at once self-evident and formidably suggestive:

> The forms of a person's thoughts are controlled by inexorable laws of pattern of which he is unconscious. These patterns are the unperceived intricate systematisations of his own language—shown readily enough by a candid comparison and contrast with other languages, especially those of a different linguistic family. His thinking itself is in a language—in English, in Sanskrit, in Chinese. And every language is a vast pattern-system, different from others, in which are culturally ordained the forms and categories by which the personality not only communicates, but also analyses nature, notices or neglects types of relationship and phenomena, channels his reasoning, and builds the house of his consciousness.

The argument is that every human being's world picture and the specific sum of such pictures in his society are a linguistic function.[21] If different cultures have different ways of mapping space and time, of qualifying motion and states of being, if a Hopi Indian can (as Whorf controversially insisted) obtain a better intuitive grasp of certain thought-pictures in Einsteinian physics than can most English-speakers, the reason is that his language has pre-

[21] This idea was, in fact, put forward for the first time by the neglected French grammarian, theosophist, and playwright Antoine Fabre d'Olivet in his *Langue hébraïque restituée* (1815–16).

pared the requisite and appropriate grooves of sensation.

Different tongues generate and program different life-forms. A given language selects particular *données*. Where Bergson and Chomsky assume *données immédiates de la conscience*, Whorf is pointing to the gradually evolving, mediate elements of culture, history, social adaptation. Each language derives certain conventions of recognition, certain rules of relationship or antithesis from a manifold, initially random or chaotic potential. Conversely, where definitions break down, where syntax dissolves, the old chaos returns, either in the pathology of an individual or in the collapse of a society.[22]

Our language is our window on life. It determines for its speaker the dimensions, perspective, and horizon of a part of the total landscape of the world. Of *a part*. No speech, however ample its vocabulary, however refined and adventurous its grammar, can organize the entire potential of experience. None, be it ever so sparse and rudimentary, fails to give *some* usable grid. The more we learn about languages, the more are we made aware of the particularity, of the vital idiosyncrasies, of any one language-vision. Thus, so much of that characteristic Western sense of time as vectored flow, of sequential causality, of the irreducible status of the individual, is inseparable from the bone-structure, from the lucid but probably over-abstract patterns of Indo-European syntax. We can locate in these patterns the substrata of past-present-future, of subject-verb-object, of pronominal disjunction between ego and collectivity, that shape so many elements in Western metaphysics, religion, and politics. Through their wealth of singular designation—their delicately graded discriminations of color, scent, and local form—through the subtle grammatical co-ordinates by which they locate different

---

[22] The thesis of "linguistic relativity," as advanced by Sapir and Whorf, is by no means generally accepted. A strong critique is presented in Max Black's *The Labyrinth of Language* (1968). For a balanced view, see F. Rossi-Landi, *"Ideologie della relatività linguistica."*

states of action at different points in space, numerous so-called "primitive" languages exploit possibilities of feeling and response which we have left fallow.[23]

To learn a language beside one's native idiom, to penetrate its syntax, is to open for oneself a second window on the landscape of being. It is to escape, even if only partially, from the confinement of the apparently obvious, from the intolerant poverty, so corrosive just because one is unconscious of it, of a single focus and monochrome lens.

The consequences for psychology are drastic. It is doubtful whether any normative, generalized psychology of the kind found, for example, in Lockeian rationalism, cuts deep enough. A psychology is topographic. It is a piece of local inventory and description, more or less complete, more or less accomplished in its techniques of excavation and projection. It maps mental operations, habits of feeling, conventions of self-awareness and "otherness" as they prevail throughout a culture or, at the largest, family of cultures. Where consciousness communicates with itself and outward in a thoroughly different linguistic context, a different psychology may be in order. There are few universals—fewer, I believe, than classic humanism and Cartesian-Chomskian models of the common man assume. Even the most "obvious," deeply incised concepts and rules of manipulation in the human psyche seem to acquire, immediately above the neurological level, local specifications and historical-cultural singularities. It may well be that there is only one universal—the incest taboo required, if it really is, for the preservation and development of the human species. Concepts of identity, of time, of the continuity or discontinuity of life and death, are not a part of Descartes' *sens commun* or a Kantian *a priori*, but highly differentiated, culturally varied, linguistically generated and transmitted conventions. Such a thing as a "universal

[23] Clyde Kluckhohn and Dorothea Leighton tell us that in the Navaho language some thousand names of plants have been recorded in current speech (*The Navaho*, 1946).

82

psychology" would have to be a branch of molecular biology. All other psychology is history of language and social usage.

Psychoanalysis provides a crucial example. Unquestionably, Freud hoped for material substantiation, for neurophysiological corroboration for his theories of mental structure. In the last analysis—and one may take the phrase as a legitimate pun—such postulates of psychoanalysis as the tripartite division of id, ego, and super-ego, or the mechanics of psychic storage, repression, and discharge, ought to be reflected in the architecture of the brain and in the neuro-chemistry of nervous impulse. Only such empirical data could support the inference of psychoanalytic universality (a point clearly seen by Malinowski when he attacked psychoanalysis from an anthropological direction in his *Sex and Repression in Savage Society*). Without physiological corroboration, the Freudian account of personality, penetrating and suggestive as it is, might remain a brilliant piece of local, historically circumscribed observation. In its awkward *bonhomie*, a remark Freud makes in *The Ego and the Id* (and it is one of numerous similar asides) shows the intensity of his search for anatomical backing: "We might add, perhaps, that the ego wears an auditory lobe—on one side only, as we learn from cerebral anatomy. . . ."

Gradually, Freud opted for a para-scientific methodology; he moved further and further from the empirical-evidential criteria of clinical psychopathology. He had to. But, in doing so, Freud entered (consciously, I think) on a Pascalian wager. The more acute his therapeutic insights, the more pressing the need for normative, experimentally verifiable neurological evidence. Without this evidence, the psychoanalytic method would become ever more an act of "personal magic," a repetition by lesser men, in a queer limbo of shamanism, of Freud's virtuoso "tricks" of insight.

It is, I believe, fair to say that the neuro-physiological

evidence has not turned up, or not in the unequivocal way expected by the early, and tenaciously hoped for by the late, Freud. Today, psychoanalysis looks more and more like an inspired construct of the historical and poetic imagination, like one of those dynamic fictions through which the master-builders of the nineteenth century—Hegel, Balzac, Auguste Comte—summarized and gave communicative force to their highly personal, dramatic readings of man and society. It is, perhaps, less as a contemporary of Poincaré or Rutherford that one now sees Freud than as the great inheritor of the nineteenth-century systematic philosophers, playwrights, and novelists. Like that of Schopenhauer, to which it has such radical affinities, the work of Freud impresses one as a superbly perceptive, eloquent summation, already tinged with a stoic premonition of incipient ruin, of European bourgeois humanism, *floruit* 1789–1914. Freud's mapping—did he himself not say "mythology"?—of human motives and behavior is profoundly circumstantial. It mirrors, it codifies rationally, the economic and social assumptions, the erotic mores, the domestic rites, of the Central European urban middle class in the years from 1880 to the collapse of agreed values in the First World War. At every point, Freud's chronicle of consciousness interacts with the surrounding sociological, economic, cultural setting. His model of libido and repression, of masculine authority, of generational antagonism, of licit and clandestine sexuality, is inseparable from the facts of family and professional existence in the Vienna of his day. There is more than a touch of buried architectural metaphor in the whole ego/id/super-ego theory—the cellarage, living quarters, and attic of the bourgeois house. Indeed, Freud's raw material and therapeutic instrument are no less verbal, no less rooted in language, than is the art of Balzac or Proust.

This is such an obvious point that it was long overlooked. Psychoanalysis is a *matter of words*—words heard, glossed, stumbled over, exchanged. There can be no analysis if the patient is mute or the doctor is deaf. There can be none, or only its indifferent rudiments, if the patient has not attained a critical level of articulateness, if his own uses of language are too thin or commonplace. If psychoanalysis has, from the outset, drawn almost exclusively on a clientèle of a very restricted social milieu, the reasons are not (or not primarily) financial and modish. Only the educated, leisured classes of society exhibit the degree of verbalization, of multiple semantic reference, of decorous elision, indispensable to the analytic process. But the question goes far beyond individual literacy. The language itself must have reached a sufficient density, a sufficient wealth of implication and effect. For psychoanalysis to function, the vernacular in which the patient freely associates must have a certain range, historical resonance, idiomatic variety, argotic underground, and body of allusion. Only then can the analyst hear inside the verbal matrix those ambiguities, concealments, word-plays, betraying muddles, on which he founds his therapeutic interpretation. (The analyst is a "translator into daylight.") In short, the particular linguistic system must be resourceful and syntactically highly evolved before the psychoanalyst's decoding can be of use.

Hence the "locality" and profoundly literary character of Freud's unravelings. These are firmly bound to the expressive and suppressive idiom of the Central European, largely Jewish middle class of the late nineteenth century in which Freud himself came of age. Freud's descriptions of the actions of consciousness and of the unconscious cannot be dissociated from the grammatical structures and referential conventions (referential especially in regard to slang and to literature) of German and Austrian German in the age of Hofmannsthal, Arthur Schnitzler, and Thomas Mann.

It may be that the psychoanalytic theory of the unconscious and of the dynamics of neurosis has general applications. But, today, it would seem that its main authority lies in the field of language-history and of the sociology of speech. No therapist since Freud has met with any true "Freudian cases"—*i.e.*, with patients whose syntax of self-consciousness and association is much like that of the men and women—more women than men—whom Freud listened to and woke echoes from in the Vienna of the 1890's. Moreover, the wide dissemination of psychoanalytic lore and literature has had its negative feed-back: much of classical Freudian praxis no longer works, precisely because the patient can no longer display the needed linguistic innocence and associative spontaneity. Too many of us now know the script in advance.

A recognition of this fact, and of the methodological dilemmas that arise from it, inspires the revaluation of psychoanalysis currently taking place in France. The pronouncements of Dr. Jacques Lacan and of the *Cahiers pour l'Analyse* are, not infrequently, indecipherably turgid and portentous. Nevertheless, their primary argument is clear and of compelling importance. *Fonction et Champ de la Parole et du Langage* and the *Propos sur la Causalité Psychique* are almost certainly the major statements made by psychoanalysis after Freud.[24] Lacan aims to re-establish the Freudian theory of psychic process and the consequent methods of therapy on a basis of linguistics. The "means of psychoanalysis are those of speech . . . its domain is that of concrete discourse." The unconscious may be understood as "a blank or a false statement" in the stream of messages through which the ego articulates its identity. Suppressed or evaded memories survive as "well-spoken lies." Indeed, memory itself is essentially a selective use of a past tense. The symptoms of neurosis can be located (*heard*) and analyzed only because they already occur "in a language form." Lacan is an ultra-nominalist: "it is the world of words that creates the world of things." Psychoanalysis is a privileged mode of insight into this creative function because it knows the semantic structure of reality,

[24] The greater part of Lacan's writings has been collected in *Ecrits* (1966).

because it knows that man is surrounded "by a total network of symbolic relations," most of which are manifest in language.

The substantive limitations of man are madness and death, conditions in which language refuses to signify. Psychoanalysis can deal with neither. (Freud's speculations on the "death-instinct" are an attempt at reintegrative myth. The "speechless" falls outside psychoanalysis precisely as it does outside Wittgenstein's factual propositions.) This is the true reason why Freudian therapy is restricted to neurosis. Neurosis operates at the level of articulate, semantically conventional, or only moderately disordered communication. Psychosis transcends grammar.

It is too soon to tell whether this attempted synthesis of Freud and of structural linguistics will work, whether it will provide psychoanalysis with the empirical backing denied to it by neuro-physiology. It may well be that, like Freud himself, Lacan is maneuvering from too narrow, too naïvely verbal a basis. The study and therapeutic uses of the media of significant communication available to the human person will have to reckon with numerous extra-linguistic codes. Known as "paralanguages," such signal-systems as gesture, mien, dance, dress, non-verbalized sound of every kind, have been much investigated since Darwin's *The Expression of the Emotions in Man and Animals* of 1872. As I stressed before, such systems do not constitute "language" and their use by modern man is, at every point, linguistically penetrated or "debased." As the work of Paget, of Kroeber, of R. L. Birdwhistell on sign languages and "kinesics" makes clear, these "paralanguages" form a kind of animate zone around the complete linguistic act.[25] But it would be surprising if an exclusively verbal approach could prove adequate to the communicative energies of the psyche, particularly of the psyche in some partial state of lesion.

[25] Cf. A. J. Greimas, ed., *Pratiques et Langages Gestuels* (*Langages*, 10, 1968).

Yet whatever the validity of Lacan's "psycho-semantics," one fact is obvious. The whole future of psychology is bound up with that of linguistic study, with our deepening grasp of man's unique speech-status. Psychology can no longer be separate from our realization of how radically a particular language, a specific linguistic world-image, conditions the life of the mind.

Already it is apparent that any fruitful study of the genesis of personality in the child is, at decisive points, a study of the development of speech and of the links between speech and conceptualization. Monkeys are less like children than behavioral psychologists or incensed parents would suppose. We are also beginning to suspect that certain patterns of *anomie*, of anti-social and anarchic conduct, are related to verbal inadequacy, to the inability of the grammatically underprivileged to "branch into" a society whose codes of communication and idiom of values are too sophisticated. Henceforth, it is unlikely that clinical and social psychology, cultural anthropology, and the study of language can get very far without constant collaboration and cross-reference. A book such as L. S. Vygotsky's *Thought and Language* (1962), written in the context of experimental psychology, points the way.

VI

Literary criticism and literary history are minor arts. We suffer at present from a spurious inflation of criticism into some kind of autonomous role. The interest wasted on the personality and quarrels of critics, the mass of criticism produced about works of literature which few of the educated public ever bother to read for themselves (T. S. Eliot on Dante is a representative case)—these are phenomena of journalism and may be indices of a general enervation. Critics and historians of literature write about writing; they offer books about books. It is nonsense to overlook this ontological derivativeness, let alone exalt the act of commentary above that of invention. Today there is even an academic *métier* in the criticism of criticism. Not very many statues are being raised to writers, but, contrary to Sainte-Beuve's gloomy prognostication, there may be before long to critics.

A plain view of the dependent, secondary nature of literary and historical comment is more than a necessary honesty. It may, in fact, open the way to a legitimate future for criticism and rescue it from some of its current triviality and megalomania.

Being words about already extant words, a discourse on modes of discourse already established, the propositions of the critic form a meta-language. That a number of literary critics have mimed in their work the expressive techniques of the text they deal with, that important literary criticism will, at times, pass into the category of "active form," does not alter the fact: criticism, analysis, *explication de texte*, commemoration (a remembering with the reader) are linguistic constructs scaffolded about a previous linguistic construct. However eloquent or poetically suggestive in statement, the critic's job of work is more truly akin to that of the logician, grammarian, and linguist than it is to that of the novelist, playwright, or poet. But precisely in that may lie the way ahead.

Every work of literature, from the barest incantations known to ethnography to the "randomized" fiction of Mr. William Burroughs, is a specialized language-act (what the latest school of criticism in France calls *écriture*).[26] It is a piece of language in a heightened condition of order, elision, reference, ornament, or phonetic expressiveness. "Literature," exactly like any act of communication, is a selection from the available totality or potential of semantic resources in a given language (or, in rare cases, more than

[26] Jacques Derrida, *De la Grammatologie* (1967), and Philippe Sollers, *Logiques* (1968), give a picture of this precious and hermetic but also stimulating approach.

89

one language). The difference being—and it can only be put roughly—that literature selects according to aims and criteria other than immediate utility and unreflective colloquialism. Literature exists only because there can be realized—again, very roughly—a membrane to divide it from the common flow of discourse. Certain lexical and syntactical material is "filtered out" according to principles other than those of basic communication. The membrane may be exceedingly thin and permeable: extreme *verismo* aims at an idiom almost completely open to the inrush of the ordinary "unselected" vulgate. But there must be a separation, a voluntary sifting according to observable criteria, for the novel, poem, or play to achieve actual being.

Once such a separation occurs—it need be no more than a modern dramatist splicing the tape he has hidden in a railway waiting-room—there results a linguistic structure, an *écriture*, of immense complexity. The number of formal variables, the range and intricacy of possible conventions, the individual, local, temporal modifiers in a literary text, are fantastic in number and specificity. By comparison, even the most taxing problems in formal logic are one-dimensional. Once it is in a condition of literature, language behaves exponentially. It is at every point more than itself. No mere inventory can exhaust the possible interactions between semantic units in even a "simple" lyric. All language, as we have seen, stands in an active, ultimately creative relationship to reality. In literature, that relationship is energized and complicated to the highest possible degree. A major poem discovers hitherto unlived life-forms and, quite literally, releases hitherto inert forces of perception. Even as Cézanne discovered the implicit but, before him, "unseen" weight and blue-shadow rotundity of apples or the patient gravamen of a chair leg.

The complexity and delicacy of the material of literature are such that neither formal logic nor linguistics has contributed more than the obvious to our understanding of a literary work. Efforts have been made to analyze the structure of poems or of paragraphs of narrative prose with the aid of symbolic logic, to dismantle the machine and locate its sources of impact.[27] Almost invariably, the outcome is an elegant diagram and a fatuous conclusion. Phonological, grammatological anatomies of literary passages are scarcely better. Their apparatus, particularly statistical, is often awesome, but the insights obtained are usually jejune and in reach of the most obvious critical reading. Neither the linguist nor the phonetician has the historical awareness, the familiarity with formal and biographical context, the training of tactile sensibility, that mark the competent critic. They lack what Coleridge called the required "speculative instruments." Because their techniques are committed to exhaustiveness, all elements must be accounted for, and to a specific degree of rigor. They must, as it were, be accounted for to several decimal places. In fact, however, formal logic and technical linguistics fall short of the provisional exactitudes of good criticism. The latter is precise, but in a very different way. Its precision may lie, for instance, in what it leaves unmapped, in the circle of diffidence it draws around the particular autonomy and "unaccountability" of the creative act. Coleridge's analysis of the nature and effects of meter in chapters XVIII and XXII of the *Biographia Litteraria*, is indirectly immediate, it proceeds tangentially to the center. It does so by mimesis, by a parallel acting out and bodying forth of meaning. The range of kinetic and nervous reference on which it draws is finely commensurate with the shape and difficulty of the question, with the fact (so often slighted by the logician) that the most polysemic of human constructs—a poem—is the object of examination.

Let us be clear. Formal logic and modern linguistics cannot do the job of the critic. But the critic, in turn, can ill afford to ignore what they, and linguistics especially, have to offer. I would go further. The current state of criti-

[27] A number of such exercises may be found in *Style in Language*, ed. T. A. Sebeok (1960).

cism is so facile and philosophically naïve, so much of literary criticism, particularly in England and America, is puffed-up book-reviewing or thinly disguised preaching, that a responsible collaboration with linguistics may prove the best hope.

Such collaboration would by no means be novel. Quintilian and the Renaissance made little operative distinction between the study of grammar and that of grammar animated by poetics or rhetoric. Negotiated via philology, an alliance between linguistics and literary criticism is explicit in the work of Eric Auerbach, Ernst Robert Curtius, and Leo Spitzer. Roman Jakobson has expounded it since 1919 and the discussions on *epitheta ornantia* by the Moscow Linguistic Circle. It underlies a good deal of the critical practice of I. A. Richards and William Empson. It was the goal of Walter Benjamin, whose "hermeneutic" readings of baroque tragedy, Goethe, and French symbolist verse relate the twentieth-century language-revolution to much older habits of Talmudic exegesis. We need not accept Jakobson's prescription [28] that linguistics be allowed to "direct the investigation of verbal art in all its compass and extent" (*direct* being the overstated term). But we must acknowledge the full force of his observation that

> the poetic resources contained in the morphological and syntactic structure of language, briefly the poetry of grammar, and its literary product, the grammar of poetry, have been seldom known to critics.

What are some of the new directions for a linguistically educated literary criticism? Obviously, a great deal wants doing in the study of the structure of poetry, in a probing, at once technical and philosophic, of the vital "strangeness," of the strictly confined yet privileged conventions of syntax, of tonal relation, which set a poem apart from all other types of signal. We need more and subtler identifica-

[28] See his key paper on "Linguistics and Poetics" (in *Style and Language*).

92

tions than are as yet available of the phonetics of poetry, of the musicality which declares, implies or dissolves meaning in a poem. In that way, to what extent is poetic "truth" made to sound true; in what manner is music the verification of poetic statement? [29] We require a congruence of historical, morphological, and literary awareness to tell us far more than we as yet know about the interactions of syntax and genre at different periods in literature. Thus, the root-energies of the heroic couplet seem to be an intensification of contemporary speech-forms, a kind of super-grammar; whereas we find in certain schools of modern verse an anti-grammar, an alternative, more contingent order of discourse than is active in normal diction.[30] What are the relations between metrical systems, between the elements of stress, recurrence, rhyme, in a given prosody and the structure of the language as a whole? Russian polysyllabic words admit only one stress and therefore enter into binary meters only if a metric stress is dropped. Does such a linguistic fact relate to the nature of the poetry produced and, in turn, to the patterns of sensibility a poetry generates in the relevant society and culture? May we think of meter as a "substitute-logic," a code of organized semantic sequences which can, but need not, mesh with the causal, temporal, spatial "rules" of ordinary discourse? What can lexical linguistics tell us of the density, of the regional or centralized focus, of the conservatism or receptivity to innovation and foreign import of a language at different stages in its history? Surely it is no longer necessary to regard as authoritative, let alone verifiable, Eliot's famous dictum that "something happened to the mind of England" between the time of Donne and that of Browning. If such a statement is to have meaning, it must be accountable to the history of the language. The true "evidence" for Eliot's theory is his own achievement as a poet;

[29] Many acute observations are contained in Christine Brooke-Rose, *A Grammar of Metaphor* (1958).
[30] Cf. Donald Davie, *Articulate Energy* (1955).

93

his own verse that is being argued here in a characteristically masked form. Indeed, Eliot's literary criticism may be the last to be so influential yet so casual in its linguistic and philosophic interest.

Beyond these lines of inquiry into the shared life of grammar, phonetics, logic, linguistic history, and poetry, there lie areas of extreme difficulty.

Do literary genres—the verse epic, the ode, verse tragedy, the prose novel—have some kind of interior life-cycle, do they correspond to needs or occasions in the language itself and lose their conviction when those occasions pass or those needs are fulfilled? What is the act of translation? What linguistic, philosophic, and poetic functions are involved when a line of poetry moves across the border from one language to another, and how is the very possibility of translation underwritten by recent models of transformational grammar? [31] If certain civilizations produce "greater," more consistently vital literature than others, is part of the reason linguistic? In other words, are some languages, in a way we cannot even formulate precisely, more suited to literary expression than others? Do their syntax and vocabulary contain a greater potential for expressive mutation, for "language set apart"? And in what way does literature generate further literature? To which question the converse would be: does the existence of a Dante, of a Shakespeare, of a Goethe in a given language inhibit the recurrence of comparable achievement? Are there entropies in language and expressive resources as there are in matter?

In 1941, John Crowe Ransom advertised: *Wanted: An Ontological Critic*, a reader equipped to disclose in poetry "the secret of its strange yet stubborn existence as a kind of discourse unlike any other." A complete ontology of poetic form and of poetic effect is very probably beyond our means. More than any other speech-act, the poem goes to the roots of language itself, to the unique communicatory

---

[31] The author is at present preparing a full-scale study of this topic.

and responsive dialectic of human identity. But advances can be made and their interest will, in Ransom's phrase, be "profounder and more elemental" than that of the majority of what now serves as literary criticism and literary history. Neither has yet registered the decisive truism that literature—all literature—is a form and function of language. It is the poets who have always known that.

VII

As we noted, the "language-revolution" arose from an urgent sense of linguistic crisis. Today, we can see how accurate Mauthner and Karl Kraus were in their alarmed foresight. Even as we are beginning to know more about language, to ask better questions about the reciprocities of speech and human identity, language itself is under pressure.

I have sought elsewhere to locate some of the main sources. Totalitarian politics, be they Fascist, Stalinist, or tribal, have set out to master language. They must do so precisely because a totalitarian model of society lays claim to the core and entirety of the human person. Modern tyrannies have re-defined words, often in a deliberate, grotesque reversal of normal meaning: life signifies death, total enslavement stands for freedom, war is peace. Stalinism and current tribal hysterias labor, often with success, to uproot the past tense from the safeguard of common remembrance. Stalinist and Maoist historiography re-invent the past. Historical occurrences, the names and very existence of human beings, unacceptable ideas, are obliterated by decree. An artifice of unanimous memory—a drilled recollection of fictions and non-events—replaces the natural plurality of individual recall. In the grammar of totalitarian speech, which Kenneth Burke [32] looked at even before George Orwell, conjugations of the verb take place

[32] See his essay "The Rhetoric of Hitler's 'Battle'" in *The Philosophy of Literary Form* (1941).

in a depersonalized present and in a utopian future (a *plus que parfait*, if I may reverse the ordinary meaning of that tense). Being a falsehood constantly altered and renewed, the past is made present. To unspeak the actual past, to eradicate the names, acts, thoughts of the unwanted dead, is a tyranny of peculiar horror. Pursued rigorously, it cuts off humanity, or certain societies, from the vital responsibilities of mourning and of justice. Man is set back in a landscape without echo.

Moreover, the planned falsification and dehumanization of language carried out by totalitarian regimes have had effects and counterparts beyond their borders. These are reflected, though in a less murderous way, in the idiom of advertisement, wish-fulfillment and consensus-propaganda of consumer technocracies. We live under a constant wash of mendacity. Millions of words tide over us with no intent of clear meaning. Quiet is becoming the prerogative of a sheltered élite or the cage of the desolate. As a result, expressive modes have been grossly inflated. Their discriminatory precision, their graphic, verifiable content have been eroded to a public smoothness. The percentage of cliché, of language-tags shared by all and lived by none, has risen steadily. A study of random samples of urban telephone calls suggests a drastic diminution and standardization of vocabulary and syntax accompanied by a formidable growth of actual speech-output. In the world of the telephone, we speak more to say less. It may be, correspondingly, that in that of radio, television, tape-recorder, and film, we hear more and listen less. Lexicographers estimate that the English tongue contains in excess of six hundred thousand words. Less than one hundred words account for seventy-five percent of all messages transmitted by telephone and telegraph. An analogous reduction of grammar, of the available delicacies and interrelations in sentence-structure, underlies the rhetoric of advertisement and mass journalism. We write fewer personal letters and our letters are shorter than in middle-class usage in the

96

eighteenth and nineteenth centuries. Our schooling puts an ever diminishing stress on verbal remembrance. How many educated individuals today can recite by heart more than a few tatters of poetry or prose? We read more in actual volume of print, but less that is exacting and linguistically enriching.[33]

If the politics of terror press on the individual, on his right to remember and to make personal statement, so do the politics of license. That the near-abolition of verbal taboos, particularly with regard to the erotic, has narrowed and weakened the imaginative authority of literature seems probable. What is more difficult to show, but more corrosive, is the effect of the removal of verbal inhibitions on the life-force, on the center and mystery of language. Saying all, and saying it in the same market-place words as everyone else, means imagining, personally re-creating, less. We face a new situation here, and one that is obviously difficult to analyze. But taboos or speech-zones reserved for occasions of special intimacy and seriousness had a vitalizing as well as a protective function.[34] Words which used to lodge at the heart of conventional silence, that were only expended in an act of complete trust and exchange of self —as sexual terms might be spoken loud in the last privacy of love—are near the deep springs of language. They kept it, in some degree, magical. Verbal reticence is the only thing that relates our publicized, exhibitionist sensibility to antique energies and sources of wonder. There was a time when the word was *Logos*, when a man would not readily deliver his true name into another man's keeping, when the name or numinous titles of the deity were left unspoken. By hounding all reserve out of our ways of speech, by making loud and public the dim places of feeling, we may be hacking up by their roots (roots, one suspects, closely related) indispensable forces both of poetry and

[33] Cf. Robert Escarpit, *La Révolution du Livre* (1965).

[34] For a rather superficial but well-informed statement, see W. Simon and J. Gagnon, "Sex Talk—Public and Private" (*Etc.*, xxv, 1968).

eros. Parading so openly, being so wastefully shared, our lives, and the language in which we experience them, go the more naked.

A more general change may be implicated in these devaluations. Ten years ago, I called it "the retreat from the word." Conceivably, verbal communication will play a smaller, a less creative role than before, in the life of consciousness. Today, non-verbal codes such as those of mathematics already map and control much of reality; soon, with a change in the sociology and criteria of literacy, they may come to communicate that reality to more and more human beings. The binomial primer, the grammar of calculus and set-theory may come to be as current as the more traditional "first reader." No word-signal can go beyond childish simile when trying to tell us that a table or a chair is a system of electrons in statistically describable motion, separated by distances and intricacies of force comparable, on their scale, to those in the galaxy. Mathematics can say this precisely and can make its statement exhilaratingly suggestive to those who know its syntax.

At many points in our immediate culture, language-forms seem stale or unwelcome, like actors from a condemned playhouse. Abstract art scorns verbal paraphrase. It demands that we learn to read its own self-contained idiom. A painting of a man in a golden helmet or of a blue bowl with red apples will, through its concentration of visual and tactile means, be "untranslatable" into any other medium; but in so far as it *represents*, as it admits of a title, the Rembrandt or Chardin canvas is an intensely "stated," syntactically organized proposition. *Black on Black* or *Composition Ninety-one* is not. A comparable advance into the absolute characterizes the abandonment of classical musical forms. A classical sonata or a romantic symphony, with its exposition, thematic development, recapitulation, and conclusion, had a marked structural analogy to the grammar of speech. The music of Stockhausen and Cage, especially where it invites a free choice of sequence, a randomization of performed units, breaks with the architecture of language. (It is precisely a dependence on ordered sequence, an impossibility of willful reversal or random placing, which, as generative grammar reminds us, constitute language.) Today, words seem to comprehend less of reality, and to tell us less of what we need to know.

So much is fairly evident. What lies further can only be conjecture.

I wonder whether the primacy of language as we have known it in human civilization, as well as many of the dominant syntactical features of language, are not the embodiment of a particular view of man's identity and death. The trinary set, past-present-future, the subject-object function, the metaphysics and psychology of the first-person pronoun, the conventions of linguistic repeatability and variation on which we found our techniques of remembrance and, hence, our culture—all these codify an image of the human person which is now under attack. A "happening," an aleatory piece of music, an artifact made only to be destroyed, are strategic denials of the future tense, even as the derision of precedent, the unsaying of history or a contemptuous indifference toward it, are a refusal of a past. In the grammar of the freak-out and the wrecker, it is always today. The idea, so crucial to our civilization, that things said and created now may, by virtue of their impertinence to the present, have a strength of being greater, scandalously more durable than our own, is seen as illusion or bourgeois hypocrisy. To the new vigilantes and utopians of the immediate, there is something outrageous in the possibility that most personal lives are insignificant and meant for oblivion, and that the present becomes future only through the music, mathematics, poetry, and thought of a very small number. Until now, an arrogant, perhaps irrational *dur désir de durer* has been the life-impulse of history. It may no longer be an acceptable ideal. The young militias are right when they bellow; the agitators are showing deep insight when they abrogate all dis-

99

cussion by saying "fuck off." They no longer share the language of their enemies. They want nothing to do with it. They would break free of language as from their own shadows. They must stop their ears to all the ceremonious, ironic voices from the past that are in books that will outlive them, and that speak of death.[35]

There is also another direction from which the individual "I," the concept of the human person as an irreducible mystery, is under pressure. Totalitarian politics, the long erosion of fear, tends to collectivize men and women, to reduce as far as possible their sanctuary of private identity. So do the conditions of standardized desire, of noise level, of programmed efficacy in a "free society." (The linguistic divergencies between West German and East German speech provide an instructive case of similar deformation under different stress.[36]) It is, today, increasingly difficult to "be oneself," to carve out for one's idiom, physical style, and habits of sensibility an untypical terrain. Under the piston-stroke of the mass media, of open and subliminal advertisement, even our dreams have grown more uniform. Like our bread, much of our manner of being comes pre-packaged. It is only in secret that we celebrate the insolent wonder of the ego, that we inhale—oh, riddle of sensuality—the smell of our own ordure.

With the development of surgical transplants, the very definition of personal existence, of a mortal, *untranslatable* self, grows perplexing. "Which part of my body was I, which will be you?" Rimbaud's *je est un autre*, that prophetic password to the trance and violence of the new freedom, is taking on a medical meaning. But it is a meaning exterior to all known co-ordinates of syntax. With heart transplantation a fact, and surgical transfers of the brain

[35] It is their understanding of the revolutionary nature of a scream and a nonsense-word which makes Jarry and Artaud the true prophets of today's insurrections.

[36] Cf. the discussion of this important topic in Hans H. Reich, *Sprache und Politik* (*Münchner Germanistische Beiträge*, I, 1968).

definitely conceivable, the *I/you* disjunction through which the language-animal entered on history is no longer self-evident.

We are in a process of profound change. I believe that the unstable, transitional status of time and personal identity, of the ego and of physiological death, will affect the authority and range of language. If these "historical universals" alter, if these syntactical foundations of perception are modified, the structures of communication will also change. Seen at this level of transformation, the much-discussed role of electronic media is only a symptom and outrider.

It would be foolish to speculate further. But let us be entirely clear about what is involved. Much of the best that we have known of man, much of that which relates the human to the humane—and our future turns on that equation—has been immediately related to the miracle of speech. Humanity and that miracle are, or have been hitherto, indivisible. Should language lose an appreciable measure of its dynamism, man will, in some radical way, be less man, less himself. Recent history and the breakdown of effective communication between enemies and generations, as it harries us now, shows what this diminution of humanity is like. There was a loud organic and animal world before man, a world full of non-human messages. There can be such a world after him. Wallace Stevens heard its premonitory signals on a winter's day:

The leaves cry. It is not a cry of divine attention,
Nor the smoke-drift of puffed-out heroes, nor
    human cry.
It is the cry of leaves that do not transcend themselves.

In the absence of fantasia, without meaning more
Than they are in the final finding of the air, in the
    thing
Itself, until, at last, the cry concerns no one at all.

TONGUES OF MEN

To the public at large, Professor Noam Chomsky, of M.I.T., is one of the most eloquent, indefatigable critics of the Vietnam war and of the role of the military-industrial complex in American life. He has marched on the Pentagon; he has supported the most extreme tactics of pacifist and conscientious dissent; he has labored to extricate his own university and the American academic community from what he judges to be its corrosive entanglements with military technology and imperialist expansion; he has run drastic professional risks on behalf of his beliefs and his intimations of catastrophe. His voice was one of the first to pillory the injustice and folly of the Vietnam operation, and it has been one of the most influential in altering the mood of educated Americans and in bringing about the drive for disengagement.

There is a second Noam Chomsky. To logicians, to behavioral psychologists, to theoreticians of child development and education, to linguists, Chomsky is one of the most interesting workers now in the field and a source of heated debate. His contributions to the study of language and mental process are highly technical and of considerable intellectual difficulty. But, like the anthropology of Lévi-Strauss, with which it shows affinities, Chomskian generative and transformational grammar is one of those specialized conjectures which, by sheer intellectual fascination and range of implication, reach out to the world of the layman. Chomsky himself, moreover, is a fluent expositor and willing publicist of his technical work; at his best, he is an "explainer" in the tradition of J. S. Mill and T. H. Huxley. Thus, a good deal of his professional argument is accessible, in part at least, to the outsider. The effort at understanding is well worth making, for if Chomsky is right, our general sense of man's habitation in reality, of the ways in which mind and world interact, will be modified or, more precisely, will join up with modes of feeling that have not had much influence or scientific weight since the seventeenth and early eighteenth centuries.

The "Chomskian revolution" pre-dates Chomsky. To a greater degree than recent disciples are always ready to acknowledge, the groundwork was laid by Chomsky's teacher, Professor Zelig Harris, of the University of Pennsylvania. Harris is himself a linguist of great distinction, and it is in his *Methods in Structural Linguistics*, which appeared in 1951, that certain key notions of grammatical depth and transformation were first set out.[1] Chomsky's

[1] The footnotes to this essay are based on comments which Noam Chomsky generously made in private communication during November, 1969.

Chomsky notes: "Harris' book was extremely important, both to the field and to me personally (I learned structural linguistics from it as an undergraduate, proofreading it, in 1947). However, it contains nothing about 'grammatical depth' or 'transformation.' Its syntax is limited to phrase-structure analysis of surface structures. Harris did begin working on a notion of transformation about 1950, within the context of his work on discourse analysis, published in two articles in *Language* in 1951. His first real article on transformations was in *Language*, 1957. . . . Harris, essentially, regards transformations as a relation defined on sentences which have been fully analyzed in terms of methods like those of his 1951 book—*i.e.*, as a kind of extension of descriptive linguistics. My own view was rather different from the start. My first work on generative grammar was an undergraduate thesis, a descriptive generative grammar of Modern Hebrew in 1949. It contains most of the ideas on generative grammar that I later worked out, with the exception of the role of transformations in syntax. Where I differed from Harris was in the conception of where transformations fit into the entire picture. For me, they were an integral part of the system for generating sentences, for giving an analytic or descriptive account in the first place."

All I would add to this valuable account is my continued belief

"Syntactic Structures," which is to many the classic and most persuasive statement of his hypotheses, followed six years later. Then, in 1958, came an important paper, "A Transformational Approach to Syntax," read at the Third Texas Conference on Problems of Linguistic Analysis in English, and "Some Methodological Remarks on Generative Grammar," published in the journal *Word* in 1961. In 1963, Chomsky contributed a severely technical and far-reaching chapter on "Formal Properties of Grammars" to Volume II of the *Handbook of Mathematical Psychology*. *Current Issues in Linguistic Theory* appeared a year later, marking the commanding prestige and wide influence of the whole Chomskian approach. *Aspects of a Theory of Syntax*, a key book, followed in 1965. *Cartesian Linguistics* (1966) is an interesting but in certain respects deliberately antiquarian salute to those French grammarians and philosophers whom Chomsky regards as his true forebears. *Language and Mind* was first delivered as the Beckman Lectures at Berkeley in January of 1967 and published a year later. It represents both a summary of generative linguistics and a program for future work. Around this core of professional writing lie explanatory or polemic interviews—notably with the English philosopher Stuart Hampshire, reprinted in the B.B.C.'s *The Listener* of May 30, 1968—and a number of lectures given in packed halls in Oxford, London, and Cambridge.

The best place to start is Chomsky's assault on Professor B. F. Skinner, of Harvard. Chomsky tells us that he paid little attention to Skinner's teachings until he himself came to M.I.T. in 1955 and saw himself compelled to take a strong position in regard to the claims of behaviorism. Skinner's *Verbal Behavior* came out in 1957. Chomsky's attack, a lengthy review in *Language*, came two years

---

that Zelig Harris' work was vital in formulating the main goals of the new linguistics. It is in Harris that we find the strong impetus toward a complete, rigorous formalization of syntactic processes. This is also the view taken by Professor J. Lyons in his recent monograph on Chomsky (1970).

later, but it had already been circulating in manuscript. What Skinner had sought to do was to extrapolate from his famous work on stimulus and response behavior in animals to human linguistic behavior. He seemed to argue that human beings acquired and made use of language in a way far more sophisticated than but not essentially different from that in which rats could be taught to thread a maze. A precise understanding and predictive theory of human speech would, therefore, involve little more than a refinement of those techniques of stimulus, reinforced stimulus, and conditioned response that enable us to teach a rat to press a certain spring in order to reach its reward of food. Concomitantly, the child would learn language skills (what Chomsky was to call "competence") by some process of stimulus and response within a Pavlovian model fully comparable to that which had proved effective, or at any rate in part, in the "teaching" of lower organisms. The qualification is needed because there is of late some doubt about what Skinner's rats have, in fact, "learned."

Chomsky found Skinner's proposals scandalous—in the restrictions they seemed to impose on the complexity and freedom of human consciousness, as well as in their methodological naïveté. Skinner's alleged scientific approach, said Chomsky, was a mere regression to discredited mentalistic psychology. It could give no true account of how human beings, *who differ in this cardinal respect from all other known life forms*, can acquire and use the infinitely complex, innovative, and at all levels creative instrument of speech. Chomsky saw—and this has, I believe, been his most penetrating insight—that a valid model of linguistic behavior must account for the extraordinary fact that all of us perpetually and effortlessly use strings and combinations of words which we have never heard before, which we have never been taught specifically, and which quite obviously do not arise in conditioned response to any identifiable stimulus in our environment. Almost from the earliest stages of his linguistic life, a child will be able to construct and to understand a fantastic number of utterances that are quite new to him yet that he somehow knows to be acceptable sentences in his language. Conversely, he will quickly demonstrate his rejection of (that is, his failure to grasp) word orders and syntactic arrangements that are unacceptable, though it may be that none of these have been specifically pointed out to him. At every stage, from earliest childhood on, the human use of language goes far beyond all "taught" or formal precedent, and far beyond the aggregate of individually acquired and stored experience. "These abilities indicate that there must be fundamental processes at work quite independently of 'feed-back' from the environment." The dynamics of human communication arise from within.

These processes, remarks Chomsky, are likely to be of enormous intricacy. They may well be located in that intermediary zone between "mental" and "physical," between "psychic" and "neuro-chemical," that our outmoded vocabulary, with its crude but deeply entrenched mind-body distinctions, is poorly equipped to handle. The child hypothesizes and processes information "in a variety of very special and apparently highly complex ways which we cannot yet describe or begin to understand, and which may be largely innate, or may develop through some sort of learning or through maturation of the nervous system." The brain produces "by an 'induction' of apparently fantastic complexity and suddenness" the rules of the relevant grammar. Thus, we recognize a new item as a sentence in our language not because it matches some familiar, previously taught item in any simple way "but because it is generated by the grammar that each individual has somehow and in some form internalized." Human language, as Chomsky was to reaffirm in 1967, is a unique phenomenon "without significant analogue in the animal world." It is senseless, contrary to what numerous biolinguists and ethnologists have felt, to theorize about its possible evolution from more primitive, outwardly conditioned modes of communication, such as the signals apparently conveyed by bird calls. The spontaneous, innovative use of language somehow defines man. It looks as if people are beings "specially designed" to generate rules of immediate linguistic understanding and construction, as if they possess "data-handling or 'hypothesis-formulating' ability of unknown character and complexity."

The vocabulary of the early Chomsky is worth a close look, particularly because its underlying thrust will be reinforced later. "Special design," "data-handling," his later references to the key "presetting" of the brain all point to the image of a computer. Chomsky would deny this, but the evidence is strong that the notion, perhaps partly unconscious, of a very powerful computer deep inside the fabric of human consciousness is relevant to much of his argument.[2] In the history of philosophy and of the natural sciences, such buried pictures or metaphors play a large role. It is doubtful whether the most recent breakthrough in molecular biology would have taken place when the Morse code was the ruling image of quick communication. The uses of "code," "feed-back," "storage," and "informa-

---

[2] Chomsky: "I wouldn't deny that the image of a computer is a live intuition for me, if by the image of a computer you refer to the abstract theory of computation—Turing machine theory, recursive function theory, finite automata theory, and the like. That has always been a very conscious model for me, and, as you perhaps know, I did a fair amount of work on certain aspects of the mathematical theory of automata, much of it summarized in my *Handbook of Mathematical Psychology* article to which you refer. But if by 'image of a computer' you mean the real, physical thing, that is neither a conscious or unconscious model for me. In fact, I've never even seen a computer, and have virtually no interest in computers. I felt, from the start, that the main effect of the availability of computers on linguistics (as on the humanities) would be to trivialize research and lead into absurd directions, and the passage of time has simply strengthened this initial guess."

Chomsky's denial stands, of course. It is for the reader of his works to judge between us. In my opinion, it is not only automata theory but the idealized image of an actual computer that underlies much of his vocabulary and of his images of the generative process. Though the issue is highly technical, it may be that Chomsky's present negative attitude toward computational linguistics reflects the failure of certain of his colleagues and disciples to produce algorithms that could be tested and re-run.

107

tion" in current genetics point to the implicit presence of computer technology and of the electronic processing of data. The same seems true of Chomskian linguistics, and this may prove important when one tries to determine whether or not they are, in fact, valid.

Chomsky's interpretation of these abilities of "unknown character and complexity" proceeds on two levels. One, highly technical, consists of an attempt to devise and describe a set of rules that will produce, or "generate," grammatical sentences in English, or any other language, and that will not produce ungrammatical ones. The other level can most fairly be termed philosophic or epistemological. Chomsky's views on generative and transformational grammars lead to certain inferences about the nature of the human mind and about the relations between being and perception. Except for purposes of study and professional formulation, these two planes of argument cannot really be kept apart. Nor ought they to be. The difficulty is that Chomsky sometimes argues as if they could, and then, at other, and often decisive, points he buttresses his formal hypotheses with inferences that are philosophic and introspective in the old, loose sense. Mathematical logic tends to overlap with hunches that are occasionally quite nebulous.

Around the turn of the century, both mathematics and logic went through a phase of rigorous self-examination. Both sought to establish formally consistent and self-contained foundations for the processes of reasoning and calculation that had developed with tremendous force in earlier centuries, but on a somewhat *ad hoc* basis. Extraordinary holes and bits of patchwork had been left in the foundations of logical and mathematical proof and analysis. The results of this house-cleaning, with which one associates thinkers such as Russell, Carnap, Tarski, and Gödel, include combinatorial logic, the theory of sets, and symbolic notations of great refinement. These tools were applied to mathematical propositions and to formal structures of logical argument. Noam Chomsky set out to apply them to the far more recalcitrant and varied material of actual human speech. (Whether he has in fact done so is one of the very difficult problems of the entire Chomskian achievement.) Only the analysis of common speech, he insisted, could lead to a genuine understanding of how language is put together.

Chomsky argued that all possible grammatical sentences in English (or any other tongue) could be derived, or "generated," from a small number of basic, or "kernel," sentences, plus a set of rules of operation and transformation.[3] We may think of these rules as in some way comparable to those surprisingly few conventions of addition, subtraction, substitution, and equivalence from which we can build up the enormously manifold and complex structure of arithmetic and algebra. Given the right manipulative rules, few building blocks are needed. The rules of Chomskian grammar "transform" certain primary configurations, such as noun symbol followed by verb symbol, into related configurations, even as algebraic equations will yield other equations if the proper rules of substitution are observed. Thus "John loves Mary" is rotated, by a transformational rule that is not only specific but also, presumably, of very comprehensive and generalizing power, into "Mary is loved by John." This particular transformation, from active to passive, allows a human speaker to

[3] "I have never used 'kernel' in this sense. Rather, the kernel sentences were (are) defined as the sentences to which only obligatory transformations have applied. No transformations at all apply to kernel sentences, but only to the abstract structures that underlie these, and all other sentences. . . . A more correct formulation would be that the base rules of the grammar generate underlying abstract (deep) structures and that transformations act upon these, converting them, step by step, ultimately into the surface structures which receive a direct interpretation in phonetic terms. The kernel sentences, then, are the sentences to which a 'minimal' sequence of transformations has applied."

I value Chomsky's clarification here, but would argue that at least three different usages of the term "kernel" can be found in his writing. Cf. the discussion of these differences in J. Lyons: *Noam Chomsky.*

109

recognize and manipulate correctly the literally innumerable number of similarly organized and related propositions that he will come up against during a lifetime. The fact that the rules for transformation are "correct" ensures that no unrecognizable, falsely or randomly ordered sentence is generated. If no such mechanism were operative, each new verbal situation—say, "I cut this loaf," "this loaf is cut by me"—would offer intractable dilemmas and demand a new, specific act of learning. This, urges Chomsky, is plainly not the case.

A sentence generated in this way has two distinct levels, and it is by virtue of this duality that Chomsky considers himself related to certain grammarians and logicians at work in France in the 1660's and after. "John loves Mary" is the *surface structure* of the sentence. It constitutes the sort of "physical signal," or phonetic articulation, to which we can perfectly well apply the traditional syntax we have learned in school: noun, verb, object, and so on. But this surface structure tells us little and obviously differs for every language. "Far below," as it were, lies the *deep structure*, from which our phonetic expression has been generated and of which the spoken, audible sentence is in some respects a projection or mapping.

What is this purported deep structure like? On this point, crucial as it is to his entire theory of language, Chomsky is elusive and not always consistent. It might have been best, though by no means satisfactory, had he said that we cannot adequately describe in words a psychic system that somehow operates before or very far beneath language. In the Kantian sense, there might be a "final skin" of consciousness and self, which we cannot describe because we cannot step outside it. Instead, Chomsky offers suggestions that are often rather obscure and tangential. The deep structure "may be highly abstract." It may or it may not have a close, "point-by-point correlation to the phonetic realization." That is, the visible contours of the landscape may or may not simulate or parallel the subterranean geological strata and dynamics from which it has been shaped and thrown up. What is worse, the visible terrain may be thoroughly misleading. Surface structures—the sentences we actually speak and hear—are not "like" the strings from which they are generated by transformational rules. The deep structures from which, according to Chomsky, our understanding and use of all languages stem involve properties of a hitherto incomprehensible generality, abstraction, and formal power. We are not, obviously, to think of these sets or primal linguistic units as verbal or syntactic in any ordinary sense. It is, if I follow Chomsky's hints rightly, *relations* that are involved—formidably simplified yet functional "presettings" that relate subject to object, person to verb. Again, I would suppose, the image of a computer, with its ability to transcribe computer rules into a print-out in English or any other idiom, is involved at some vital though perhaps unacknowledged stage in Chomsky's argument.

In any case, what has been shown is this: the unbounded variety of sentences human beings grasp and make use of at every occasion in their lives can be derived from a limited set of formal counters and from a body of rules, also presumably limited, for the manipulation and rearrangement of these counters. To have shown this—and I think Chomsky has done so—is of itself a feat of great logical force and elegance. Substantively as well as historically, the exemplary suggestion came from mathematics and mathematical logic. In the binary system of notation, for instance, two symbols, 0 and 1, together with a body of rules about how they are to be put together and "read," suffices to set down and operate with any number or group of numbers in the universe. Logic strives for a comparable economy and rigor at the base. Chomsky's hope that human language can be similarly schematized is understandable and intellectually exciting. But there is more to it than that. Chomsky is not arguing a mathematical model, a *hypothesis*—as Renaissance scientists called any of those formal proposals to which they did not necessarily attach material truth. Chomsky addresses himself to the human fact. He contends that only some such scheme of generation and transformation out of deep structures can account for the way in which *Homo sapiens* actually acquires language and communicates. He summarized this connection in his first Locke Lecture, at Oxford:

> A person who knows a language has mastered a set of rules and principles that determine an infinite, discrete set of sentences each of which has a fixed form and a fixed meaning or meaning-potential. Even at the lowest levels of intelligence, the characteristic use of this knowledge is free and creative . . . in that one can instantaneously interpret an indefinitely large range of utterances, with no feeling of unfamiliarity or strangeness.

The postulate that language is unique to man (with which I entirely concur) and the correlative notion of a *deep structure* have wide philosophic consequences. Of late, Chomsky has been readier than before to examine these and to move outside the confines of formal linguistic analysis. The key question is that of the nature and location of these deep structures and of the process through which human beings have achieved their singular capacity to articulate meaning and express imaginary concepts. In his attack on Skinner, Chomsky stressed the "completely unknown" character of the whole business and admitted that it might result from some form of learning or from a gradual maturation of the nervous system. But, as his hypotheses have gained confidence and prestige, Chomsky has come to adopt what he himself calls a Cartesian position but what might more exactly be termed a development of Kant's theories of perception.

It is innate ideas or innate programs for all potential experience that Chomsky is inferring. The existence of an "innate mental structure" seems to him indispensable to the generation of language. The "schema of universal grammar," whereby all men can operate in their own tongue and reasonably acquire another, must be assigned "to the mind as an innate character." Knowledge of language can be gained only "by an organism that is preset." Only man is innately equipped or programmed in this immensely specific yet creative fashion. All men being thus organized, there exists between them the bond of universal grammar and the concomitant possibility of translation from any one language into all other languages.[4] It follows as well that no lower organic species will be able to master even rudimentary language forms (which is rather different from saying that certain animals may not be taught to mime human speech sounds). As Chomsky notes, recent studies of animal vision suggest that various species see angle, motion, and other complex properties of the physical world according to the special ways in which their nervous systems are patterned or "hooked up." These patterns are innate, and unalterable except through artificial lesion. Precisely in the same way, man communicates reality to himself and to others in linguistic forms because he has been uniquely imprinted with the capacity and need to do so.

---

[4] "The existence of universal grammar, in my sense," says Chomsky, "carries no 'concomitant possibility of translation from any language into all other languages.' This fact, and the reasons for it, are discussed specifically in *Aspects of the Theory of Syntax* (1965)—e.g., p. 30, where I point out that 'the existence of deep-seated formal universals . . . does not . . . imply that there must be some reasonable procedure for translating between languages.' Critical is the distinction between formal and substantive universals, discussed there at some length."

Here, our differences are fundamental. The relevant passages in *Aspects* (and notably the long footnote on pp. 201–2) seem to me to constitute a *non sequitur* and one of the decisive flaws in the Chomskian "universalist" case. As Leibniz clearly saw, a postulate of deep-structured linguistic universality *must* entail a reasonable procedure for translation between different languages. In fact, it must entail a formal procedure, even if the latter remains an unattained ideal. The distinction offered by Chomsky as between "formal" and "substantive" universals does not help. If they are "that formal," what can they tell us of actual language and of the profoundly important, difficult problem of linguistic multiplicity? I am now engaged on a full-length study of this problem and of the light it may throw on a theory of language.

113

We are back with Kant and those *a priori* mental structures or categories of space, time, and identity through which man interacts with the "outside" world and which govern both the freedom and the conceptual limits of that interaction. We are also back with the doctrines of the great grammarians of Port Royal in the second half of the seventeenth century regarding the universal grammar from which all human tongues ultimately derive their local forms.

How far can we probe into these deep structures and "settings" of consciousness? What kind of evidence are we looking for? Again, Chomsky is elusive and inclines toward modest disclaimers: "In fact, the processes by which the human mind achieved its present stage of complexity and its particular form of innate organization are a total mystery, as much so as the analogous questions about the physical or mental organizations of any other complex organism." Inasmuch as Chomsky has just drawn, and shrewdly so, on the positive results being achieved in the study of animal perception, this rider to the sentence is odd.[5] Elsewhere, moreover, he is less circumspect. Lin-

---

[5] "Three entirely separate matters are involved," objects Chomsky. "First, deep structure. Second, innate structures of mind ('settings of consciousness'). Third, the matter of 'evolution' of innate structures of mind. As to the first, we can probe quite extensively into deep structures, and I and others have done so in our descriptive work in transformational generative grammar. You ask 'what kind of evidence are we looking for.' In connection with deep structures, the answer is straightforward in principle, though there are serious empirical problems. A TG contains base rules and transformational rules; the deep structures are those generated by the base, and converted to surface structures by transformation; the evidence that we are looking for is empirical evidence bearing on the correctness of one or another hypothesis about the choice and interrelation of base and transformational rules; the evidence ultimately involves the sound and meaning of sentences, intuitions regarding deviance, pairing of sound and meaning, and so on. . . .
"The second matter, innate structures, is different in content, but the same general remarks apply. The empirical issue is straightforward. Given that competence is correctly described by a TG grammar (an empirical assumption itself, of course), we face the empirical issue of designing an abstract 'language acquisition device' with the following property: given data of the sort available to the language-learner, it constructs the descriptively adequate

114

(the true) generative grammar. The internal structure of this device (call it LAD) is the system of innate principles and structures which we attribute to the human mind, as an empirical hypothesis. LAD must meet two kinds of conditions: it must be rich enough in structure so that it produces the correct generative grammar on the basis of the actual data available; it must be loose enough in structure to permit the actual diversity of known, and humanly possible, languages. In principle, the question is straightforward; the difficulties and problems are, again, empirical, and there has been a good deal of progress. Notice, incidentally, that there is no logical connection between deep structures and innate structures. . . .

"The third question has to do with the 'processes by which the human mind achieved its present stage. . . .' Here I think we know nothing at all. My 'elusiveness' and 'modest disclaimers' have to do with this issue, the issue of evolution and emergence and the physical principles that govern these processes. The 'rider' you quote is not, as you say, 'odd,' but is rather a simple recognition of the fact that molecular biology, ethology, the theory of evolution, and so on, have absolutely nothing to say about this matter, beyond the most trivial observations. And on this issue—though not the first two matters that are confused with it—linguistics has nothing to say either."

A thorough investigation of these points would, of itself, require a full-length essay. But the areas of disagreement are clear. Problems which Chomsky characterizes as "straightforward" and "empirical" seem to me to be fundamental and philosophic. Even if it is taken as an abstract idealization, the scheme of a total formalized account of grammar is reductive in the extreme, and probably misconceived. The open-ended, dynamic, ontologically temporal nature of the human experience of language militates against this order of total and normative description. Primary determinants of "correctness," to cite only one obvious example, are subject only to intuitive or partial recognition. For closely argued developments of this point, cf. Willard Van Orman Quine: *Word and Object* (1960), chapters ii–iv, and I. A. Richards: *So Much Nearer* (1968), chapter iv.

I am equally troubled over the connections or lack of "logical" connections between deep and innate structures. What is the relation of this "parallel" model to the key claim of universality? When Chomsky cites the work he published with Morris Halle in 1968 on the *Sound Pattern of English* as containing the "most exciting results on universal grammar" so far produced, he points to what most linguists regard as the weakest part of the transformational generative case. As phoneticians pointed out, the examples offered by Chomsky and Halle did not, in many cases, apply even to "English" as distinct from "American" English. It is here, where the issues of "depth," "innateness," and "universality" conjoin—issues which are so evidently philosophic and psychological—that the Chomskian picture of the mind appears least convincing.

As I point out in other papers in this collection, I disagree with Chomsky's dismissive ruling on the relations between linguistics and certain aspects of biological and evolutionary theory. Observations already made, at points where these disciplines or modes of argument meet, seem far from trivial. Moreover, even if Chomsky's pessimism should prove justified, even if the study of language and guistic universals, says Chomsky to Stuart Hampshire, must "be a biological property of the human mind." He adds, in a move strikingly reminiscent of those made by Freud when he was hoping for neuro-physiological confirmation of his model of the subconscious (confirmation that never came), that there will "definitely someday be a physiological explanation for the mental processes that we are now discovering."

Does this confident assertion signify that generative linguistics is committed to materialism, to a view of consciousness as being purely and simply neuro-chemical? Some of its adherents seem to believe so. Chomsky's own formulation is subtler. He rightly points out that the boundaries between "mental" and "physical" are continually shifting. Numerous phenomena once regarded as wholly spiritual and outside the reach of empirical study have now become comprehensible in a physiological and experimental sense. There is beginning to be a chemistry of schizophrenia and a biochemistry of dreams, as there has for some time now been a physiology of digestion or procreation. It is by keeping our descriptive categories open and negotiable that we can extend knowledge. "What is at issue," says Chomsky, "is only whether the physiological processes and physical processes that we now understand are already rich enough in principle—and maybe in fact—to cover the mental phenomena which are beginning to emerge" (again, the phrasing might be Freud's). The work done in the past fifteen years on the genetic code and on the neuro-chemistry of nervous impulse goes a long way toward suggesting how fantastically complicated and creative the energies at work in organic molecular processes are. The development of

---

of human evolution should fail to interact, such failure would be no small or obvious matter. A theory of the innateness and generation of language in man which has no substantive regard to the biological, evolutionary, social aspects of the phenomenon will remain necessarily arbitrary and incomplete. It can be of supreme formal power and logical acuity (as so much of Chomsky's early, best work is). But it runs a deepening risk of triviality. Our disagreement here is, I believe, fundamental.

such work may—though Chomsky is saying that it very well may not—lead to some understanding of the "anatomy" of innate deep structures and linguistic generation.

II

In a simplified, obviously abbreviated form, these are the theories Professor Chomsky has put forward over the last twelve years. No one since the great French-Swiss linguist Saussure, in the early part of the century, and I. A. Richards, in the 1930's, has had more impact on the study of language or done more to suggest that linguistics is indeed a central discipline in the understanding of mind and behavior. But this does not mean that Chomsky's views have been universally accepted. They have been sharply queried by other linguists, and there are some signs that the Chomskian wave may be receding. That such a recession might occur at a moment when Chomsky's ideas are receiving their widest public and "journalistic" echo would be a coincidence common in the history of science and of ideas.

A good deal of the controversy in the profession is of an extremely technical nature. It involves differences of approach in regard to combinatorial logic, mathematical psychology, and semantics which are scarcely accessible to the layman. Nevertheless, a number of salient doubts can be made out. These are stated with great penetration by Professor Charles F. Hockett, of Cornell, in *The State of the Art* (1968). Hockett rejects the whole Chomskian model of the generation of grammatical sentences from hidden finite sets and rules. Chomsky's picture of language, says Hockett, is absurdly over-abstract; it is a fiction patterned not on real human speech but on the artificial propositions and tautologies of formal logic. Hockett's way of putting this decisive point is arduous but unmistakable: a mathematical linguistics on Chomskian lines is an absurd-

117

ity because human speech is not a "well-defined subset of the set of all finite strings over a well-defined alphabet." In simpler terms: when we deal with human speech, we are not dealing with a rigorously definable, closed system all of whose variants can be derived from a single set or cluster of unchanging elements. We are not looking at a table of chemical elements all of whose structures and atomic weights can be reduced to combinations of certain primal, strictly defined units. Chomsky's transformational grammar fails to account for the vital, fascinating ability of human speakers not only to know how to string words together to form a sentence but to know when and how to *stop*. This is one of those apparently obvious but deep points on which the cogency of a theory of language may well depend. Let me make it as plain as I can. "One plus one equals two" is a completely acceptable English sentence. "One plus one plus one equals three" is already faintly awkward and almost implies a didactic or special context. "One plus one plus one plus one equals four" is intolerable, and so will be all further sentences built on the same pattern. Yet, formally, all such sentences are transformations of the first by virtue, presumably, of the "additive rule" somehow established in the passage from deep to surface structure. Nothing is *grammatically* wrong with a string of ones connected by "ands" or "pluses." Yet we know, and know at an early, precise point, that we are no longer speaking acceptable English, that we are at best apeing a computer language. What gives us this definite but extraordinarily subtle, perhaps "musical," knowledge? [6]

[6] Chomsky rejects this point entirely: "Our knowledge of language determines a precise phonetic form and semantic representation for indefinitely many sentences which, for various reasons, we would never say. This is the fact (one of the facts) that a linguistic description must account for. . . . I really think you haven't thought through this matter properly. You're quite right in saying that a grammar does not generate 'acceptable English.' That is not its intention. As discussed in detail in *Aspects*, there is a fundamental conceptual difference between what I call there 'acceptability' and 'grammaticalness.' "
I accept Chomsky's correction as to the full force of Hockett's

There is no genuine evidence, argues Hockett, for anything like the deep structures that Chomsky postulates. There is, on the contrary, plenty of evidence that different languages handle the world in very different ways and that all languages have in them "sources of openness" that Chomsky ignores. His fundamental error, urges Hockett, is the belief that a study of semantics can ever be separated from a study of the actual grammar and lexicon of the relevant language or family of languages. By patient comparison of languages as they are in fact spoken, and by careful induction, we may come to discover "cross-language generalizations." J. Greenberg's *Universals of Language*, published in 1963, and comparative analyses of Southwest American Indian languages now in progress, are steps in the proper direction. The empirically located and verified common traits or language habits that emerge from this kind of ethno-linguistic study may have nothing to do with universal deep structures. A universal grammar in Chomsky's sense is, according to Hockett, a pipe dream. It is not universal kernel sentences and transformational rules but a manifold context of specific political history and social sensibility that make a man "stand" for office in English English and "run" for it in American.[7]

point. But the issue is again a complex one. The formal distinction as made in *Aspects* is clear. But when applied to actual language, especially by Chomsky's disciples, "acceptability" and "grammaticalness" overlap constantly, the one being used to determine the other. In my own view, *both* are relativistic, largely intuitive categories subject to historical and social alteration. On this entire question, transformational generative linguistics seems to be using evidence in a circular way.

[7] Chomsky strongly argues that almost all comparative analyses of linguistic structures made up to now are "superficial" and "hopelessly elementary." What is needed is "serious comparative work that tries to operate in the only logically appropriate way, namely, by constructing descriptive adequate grammars of a variety of languages and then proceeding to determine what universal principles constrain them, what universal principles can serve to explain the particular form that they have. Thus I think of Hugh Matthews' grammar of Hidatsa, the most detailed grammar so far of any American Indian language, Paul Postal's work on Mohawk, Ken Hale's beautiful studies of Papago and Walbiri and other Southwest Indian and Australian languages, Stanley's work on Navajo,

Hockett's charge that Chomsky leaves out the spontaneous, altering genius of actual speech touches on a larger philosophic dissent. This is well put by Dr. Yorick Wilks in a recent review of *Language and Mind*. Wilks suggests that, despite all its acerbity and conviction, Chomsky's quarrel with Skinner is a trifle spurious. The dispute is not between a mechanistic model and a free or idealistic vision of the production of human speech, but "between two alternative mechanistic theories: Skinner's the simple one, and Chomsky's the more complicated." In the terms I have been using, the quarrel would be between a model based on an

---

and much more. . . . I think if you take a careful look at what is really being done in the field now, you will discover that a good part of the comparative work, and the part that penetrates by far the most deeply into the structure of specific languages, is being done within the TG model, and with the conscious goal of exploring properties of universal grammar."

No disagreement so far as the work cited goes. I would only add that the "construction of descriptively adequate grammars of a variety of languages" is a far more difficult—philosophically difficult—job than Chomsky's program suggests. Whether such a grammar exists for Latin, let alone English, is a moot point. Furthermore, such construction will, I think, implicate precisely those areas of historical, re-creative intuition and "non-formality" which the TG model excludes.

But the worry lies deeper. So far as I am aware, Chomsky has until now offered only one example of a genuine formal universal (*Aspects*, p. 180). It concerns the rules which govern the operations and legitimacy of deletion in the underlying structure of sentences of the type "I know several more succesful lawyers than Bill." These "erasure transformations" may be proposed for "consideration as a linguistic universal, admittedly on rather slender evidence." I am not even certain that all Chomskians would subscribe to this example. In *Universals in Linguistic Theory* (1968), E. Bach urges the study of "even deeper and more abstract structures," of "abstract kinds of pro-verbs which receive only indirect phonological representation." How is any student "from outside" or informer "within" a language to discover and compare "universal principles" of this order? The Chomskian program, fascinating and attractive as it is, may be setting out to explore what it has already postulated. Robert A. Hall's guarded conclusion seems closer to the facts: "Linguistic structures do differ, very widely indeed, among all the attested languages of the earth, and so do the semantic relationships which are associated with linguistic structures. . . . It is still premature to expect that we can make any except the most elementary observations concerning linguistic universals and expect them to be permanently valid. Our knowledge of two-thirds or more of the world's languages is still too scanty (or, in many instances, nonexistent)."

120

old-fashioned adding machine and one founded on a super-computer. Wilks then argues that the kind of mechanistic scheme devised by the behaviorists would, if sufficiently refined, produce the types of basic sentences and transformations posited by Chomskian grammar. That is—and this is a penetrating observation—the language picture postulated by Chomsky does not depend necessarily or uniquely on the theory of generation from deep structures. What were called "finite-state" and "phrase-structure" rules of grammar could also do the job: "If anyone came in and watched the two machines chugging away, he could never tell that they had been programmed with quite different rules."

How can we ever hope to look "inside the machine" (an image as Cartesian as it is Chomskian)? Chomsky's "innate structures," says Dr. Wilks, may well represent a "retreat from the facts," a refusal to submit his formal design to any possibility of experimental investigation. How can we expect to find out *what* is innate in the mind? "We can't look; external behavior is no guide at all, and, of course, it's no help to ask what people think." In view of this impenetrability of innate "presettings," it is a very odd step, suggests Wilks, to pass from categories of grammatical description that may be "natural" and "deep" in Western languages to the assertion that there are universal mental patterns underlying *all* languages. How can we assign to languages profoundly different from ours innate grammatical properties obviously patterned on our own habits of syntax? Chomsky may, almost inadvertently, be tending toward a mechanistic doctrine of his own, all the more disturbing in that it would be culturally as well as formally deterministic. Though Wilks does not make the point, the radical humanism of Chomsky's politics would render such a position deeply ironic.[8]

[8] Chomsky's refutation of this point seems to me entirely right. I had misinterpreted him: "a radical humanism should develop within a theory of the 'human essence' that involves innate struc-

Dr. Wilks's point relates immediately to my own main difficulties in regard to Chomsky's theory of language. Some four thousand languages are in current use on our crowded planet. There are numerous territories in Africa, Asia, and Latin America (not to mention corners of Switzerland) that are splintered by distinct, mutually incomprehensible tongues, though these territories are uniform in climate, way of life, and economic needs. These four thousand languages, moreover, are almost certainly the remnants of an even greater number. So-called rare languages disappear every year from active usage and the recollection of aged or isolated informants. This proliferation of human idiom is an immensely exciting but also scandalous fact. Few linguists since Wilhelm von Humboldt, in the early decades of the nineteenth century, have thought hard enough about its enigmatic implications. Today, the professional divisions between formal, mathematical linguistics (if such really exist), on the one hand, and the comparative and anthropological study of actual languages, on the other, have further blurred the issue. I am unable to consider intellectually satisfactory or adequate to the truth any model or formula of human verbal behavior that does not in some way account for this fantastic multiplicity. Why four thousand or more languages? Why, by a factor of a thousand, more languages than, say, there are human races or blood types? No Darwinian analogy of variation through natural selection and adaptation will do. The vast variety of fauna and flora represents a wealth of specific adjustment to local conditions and to the requirements of competitive survival. The opposite is true of the proliferation of neighboring tongues. That proliferation has been one of the most evident and intractable barriers to human collabora-

---

tures of mind. So it seems to me. I think, incidentally, that Bakunin (for one) was sadly in error on this point, and that much of modern ideology is also enormously confused, in its rather thoughtless association of reaction with nativism, progressive ideology with empiricism."

tion and economic progress. It has left major areas of human habitation internally riven and largely isolated from history. Many cultures that have come to stagnation or ruin may have been linguistic dropouts—which is not to say that we have any solid evidence that one language is better suited than another to the realization of individual or social achievement. We know of no people that does not have in its mythology some variant on the story of the Tower of Babel. This is eloquent proof of men's bewilderment in the face of the multiplicity of tongues that has set between them constant walls of seeming gibberish and silence. Translation is not a victory but a perpetual, often baffling necessity.

To my mind, it is now the main job of linguistics, working with anthropology and ethnography, to get our actual language condition into clear focus. (We do not even have a truly exhaustive language atlas as yet.) We must learn to ask the right questions about the deeply puzzling phenomenon of linguistic diversity.

The fundamental matter of language proliferation hardly turns up in this way in the theory of generative and transformational grammar. A cryptic remark occurs toward the close of *Language and Mind:* "The empirical study of linguistic universals has led to the formulation of highly restrictive and, I believe, quite plausible hypotheses concerning the possible variety of human languages." First of all, it is a moot point whether this is so. The preliminary investigation of what certain linguists provisionally assume to be syntactic universals has until now been limited to but a few languages, and the results obtained have been at an almost intangible level of generality (*i.e.*, "in all known languages there are verbs or parts of speech that indicate action"). But let us suppose that the kind of empirical study which transformational generative linguists and others are pursuing does in fact produce verifiable "cross-language generalizations." These would not necessarily support Chomsky's theory of universal grammar and in-

123

nate deep structures. The point is crucial and must be put carefully.

Chomsky postulates "innate presettings" deeply embedded or imprinted in the human mind. They "must simply be a biological property." Now, such settings *could* lead to the production, through transformational rules, of thousands of human languages. They could, but there is absolutely no obvious reason for them to do so. On the contrary: given a scheme of base structures and functional rules, complex but certainly finite, we would expect the generation of a very restricted, clearly interrelated number of human tongues. What we *should* find, if the Chomskian theory of innate biological universals is true, is the order of diversity shown by human pigmentation and bone structure. The degree of variety here is totally different, both qualitatively and quantitatively, from that which we find in language. Let me go further: the linguistics of Noam Chomsky *could* account, and could account with beautiful economy and depth, for a world in which men would all be speaking *one* language, diversified at most by a moderate range of dialects. The fact that generative and transformational grammar would be beautifully concordant with such a result, that such a result is in some manner both natural and obvious to Chomsky's postulates, seems to me to cast serious doubts on the whole model. Like the great language mystics, who extend from Nicholas of Cusa to Jakob Boehme, Chomsky often seems to conjure up the radiant fiction of that single tongue spoken by Adam and his sons but forever lost and pulverized at Babel. In short, key features of the Chomskian language revolution appear to go against the grain of the linguistic situation in which the human race actually finds itself and in which it has existed so far as history and conjecture can reach back.[9]

---

[9] Chomsky qualifies my remarks at this stage as "irresponsible." He states that "What we would expect, given the theory of formal and substantive universals, is a tremendous diversity of mutually unintelligible languages, all satisfying the same, fixed set of deep,

The controversies initiated by Chomsky's own polemics against behaviorism are only in their early phase. It may be that the arguments urged against universal grammar will be met and that the notion of deep structures will acquire better philosophic or physiological support. Recently, claims have been put forward suggesting that children between the ages of eighteen months and two years formulate sentences in a way that exhibits deep structures not yet overlaid by any particular language. Notably, it has been claimed that there are Chomskian analogues in the way in which Russian and Japanese children acquire their respective languages. Here indeed would be the kind of concrete evidence that is being widely awaited. Time and investigation may tell. One thing is clear: Chomsky is an exhilarating thinker, possessed, as was Spinoza before him, by a passionate appetite for unity, for complete logic and explanation. There is a common bond of monism in Chomsky's desire to get to the root of things, be they political or linguistic. But it might be, to advance a cautionary platitude, that neither politics nor language is quite like that. Unreason and the obstinate disorder of local fact may prove resistant to the claims of either political justice or formal logic. It is part of the stature of Chomsky's work that the issues of disagreement raised by it are basic. To me, man looks a queerer, more diverse beast than Chomsky would have him. And Nimrod's tower lies broken still.

---

invariant, highly restrictive principles. And the evidence indicates that this is exactly what we do find."

We disagree—sharply, it would appear—over the amount and quality of "evidence" forthcoming. To me, the matter of "tremendous diversity" and "mutual unintelligibility" is basic to any theory of human speech and of how such speech may have evolved. I suspect that Chomsky would regard as merely "of the surface" questions which seem to be primary and ontological. This is precisely the starting point for work toward a theory of translation.

LINGUISTICS AND
POETICS

T he naked truism that "all literature is language" states both the self-evidence and the great difficulty of the argument. *All* literature—oral or written, lyric or prosaic, archaic or modern—is language in a condition of special use. Every literary form—the incantation of the Bushman or a *nouveau roman*, a rhyming doggerel on the lavatory wall or St. John of the Cross's "Songs of the soul in rapture at having arrived at the height of perfection, which is union with God, by the road of spiritual negation," *King Lear* or *The Mousetrap*—is no more and no less than a language act, a combination of syntactic units. There can, conceivably, be language without literature (artificial or computer languages may satisfy this negative condition): there can be no literature without language. Mallarmé's dictum that poems are made not of ideas but of *words* cuts deep.

Literature is "language in a condition of special use." Here our difficulties begin. What is that condition? No articulate statement, one might almost say, no phonetic act or inscription but is susceptible of communicating emotion and, in a sustaining context, of conveying a sense of governed form. All signals we emit are potentially resonant with values and intensities beyond those of bare information. Zola made gross but memorable art of an inventory of cheeses; Joyce could, I imagine, spin music off a random page in the telephone directory. In short: we cannot, *a priori*, point to any language act or element and say: "this is excluded from all literary employ." Indeed, in the precise sense figured in Borges' allegory of the Library at Babel, that "library which others call the Universe," all literature—Aeschylus and Dante, Shakespeare and Tolstoy, as well as the masters not yet born—is extant, is latent life, in the mere mechanical aggregate of language. It is no more than a certain combination of words, potentially available as are *all* combinations, in the total vocabulary and grammatical sets of a given tongue.

Yet, in some vital measure, this combination is realized according to criteria different from, or at the least not wholly corresponding to, criteria of immediate speech (we have to be very careful here because it is precisely the criteria of immediate, unselected speech that certain literary genres of naturalism or *verismo* seem to simulate). The poet, the "maker of literature," chooses his linguistic material from the totality of available expressive means. So, of course, does anyone formulating a sentence or even a monosyllabic outcry. But the poet's selection occurs at a special level of deliberation. It stems from a special intensity of conscious focus. Many—in fact, most—of the pertinent indicators are common to the poet and to anyone in his society who would speak with clarity, force, personal stress, and a minimal elegance. All good speech has in it energies which are poetical. In poetry, except at the extreme limits of esoteric or nonsense verse, the main strengths are those of common expressiveness. But the literary intent is, at its obscure but primary root, different. Literature is language freed from a paramount responsibility to information ("paramount" is necessary because much great literature, from Hesiod's *Works and Days* to Solzhenitsyn's *The First Circle*, is meant to inform in ways entirely comparable to those of a treatise on agronomy or of a newspaper article). The paramount responsibilities of literature, its ontology or *raison d'être*, lie outside immediate utility and/or verifiability. But note how difficulties bristle: the immense moral, psychological "utility" of literature is a commonplace—though one which I feel needs re-examining—and the "truths" discovered and communicated by great art are among the best we hold. I mean something more banal: the poem or the novel may prove of extraordinary use to the community; the propositions it puts forward about life may be authentic and of the deepest validity. But these benefits will, as it were, be ancillary. We do not turn to literary form at the first brute need of communication; there is always a simpler way of saying things than that of the poet. Perhaps speed is relevant here: literature is more prodigal of time than is unpremeditated statement. Like music, it moves in temporal co-ordinates which are, in some tangible but difficult to define way, proper to itself. Both the prolixities and concisions of literary language have metronome markings which differ from those of the routine and largely indiscriminate currents of common verbal exchange.

Hence, I believe, the profound, obsessive striving of the poet after survival: literature is language in some degree outside ordinary time; it will survive time better, say Ovid, than marble or bronze. And the truths which it states, while being no less rigorous, no less important, no less radical than those stated by an historical document or mathematical theorem, are not subject to quite the same modes of proof. When literature is most itself, the sum of truth and information which is inherent in it cannot be abstracted, cannot—or can only very imperfectly—be paraphrased. The particular truth and information are indivisible from the exact combination of formal expressive devices, from the unique enacted or "executive form" (R. P. Blackmur's term) of the given ode, sonnet, drama, or fiction. In common speech, a major proportion of linguistic material is contingent, superfluous, merely conventional; neighboring or roughly analogous counters can be substituted and little will be lost. Ideally—and there is much

of that degree of the ideal in Dante, in Keats, in a paragraph by Proust—a single alteration will transform or
destroy the literary text. It will change the life of meaning.
A poetic form *acts out* its meaning, and is as inseparable
from the complete formal motions of that action as is, in
Yeats's famous query, the dancer from the dance.

Let me go back to the start. Literature is language, but
language in a condition of special use: that condition being
one of total significance, and of a significance which is—
for every true poem or piece of literary prose—unique. No
replacement of any semantic element, however small (consider the role of typography in Mallarmé, in e. e. cum-
mings) will do. These two criteria seem to allow a rough,
working measurement of the distance between literature
and the language-world or lexical and syntactic context
from which it is drawn.

But even as literature is at every moment and by definition drawn from the history and currency of the relevant
language, so our understanding of literature is, in essence,
linguistic.

To classical antiquity this was a truism. So far as antiquity conceived of "literature" at all (and whether and
how early it did so remains a moot point), it saw the
métier of the poet or tragedian as being one of special
appliance: language applied, in a perfectly deliberate
and analyzable fashion, to the job or persuasion, instruction, ornamentation or dissimulation, as the case might be.
Poetics came under the heading of rhetoric; both were
patently of the realm of the grammarian and teachers of
eloquent discourse. In political societies in which the arts
of government and public management were very largely
those of persuasive formulation, the poet was supreme
exemplar of efficient speech. In Homer a man might find
tags to organize for himself, borrowing terms unmatched
for economy and musical memorability, almost any posture
of civic, military and domestic experience. Out of Euripides on rage, on eros, on the coming of a storm, the

speaker in the city would learn how to align most effectively the tonal, plastic and grammatical resources of daily usage. The grammarian parsing the *Iliad* to generations of schoolboys, the scholiast on Sophocles, were, in the fullest sense, applied linguists, "pointers out" of the joints and bevels with which the master carpenters of the language had put together notable linguistic artifacts. That there might be, as Plato argued in the *Ion*, mysterious, daemonic sources of impulse at work in the poet's creative frenzy did not in any way subtract from the essentially rhetorical, rationally demonstrable anatomy of his product. At only one major point did the classical view of poetry and drama touch on genuinely fundamental issues of the nature of language. This was in the conflict between the Platonic theory of *mimesis* and the Aristotelian model of *katharsis*. The Platonic notion of the capacity of language, particularly when joined to music, to elicit imitative action, his insight into the possibility that verbal fictions weaken or corrupt our grasp on what Freud was to call "the reality principle," his attempt to distinguish negatively between verifiable and poetic truths—all these raise linguistic issues of final importance. Aristotle's rejoinder is based on a far less penetrating sense of language and inclines to a cursory identification of form with explicit content. Nevertheless, in the *Poetics* no less than in the *Ion* and the *Republic*, questions regarding the operations of language are posed, or at least intimated, which have not, until now, been resolved. For the rest, the poetics of antiquity are, resolutely, a branch of the study of grammar and public discourse. Via Cicero and Quintilian, this classification obtains throughout medieval and scholastic study of the written word.

Hugues de Saint-Victor's *Didascalicon*, with its significant subtitle *De studio legendi* ("an art of reading"), dating from the first half of the twelfth century, is a well-known case in point. The commanding rubric is that of *logica*, the study both analytic and heuristic of the proper laws and effective conventions of human speech, when that speech is purged of the randomness and anarchy of vulgate usage. The analysis of grammar leads to that of argument (*logica dissertiva vel rationalis*), demonstration, dialectic and invention being the natural aims of thoroughly mastered, organized linguistic structures. *Rhetorica* is a subspecies of this threefold division, as literature and secular eloquence are special cases of persuasive and ornamented dialectic.

These neo-Aristotelian or post-Hellenistic taxonomies may strike us as arbitrary or imperceptive. But they brought with them a scruple and a strength of actual linguistic practice which constitute one of the real, and all but extinct, glories of the Western inquisitive tradition. Exegetists from the twelfth century to Scaliger possessed a knowledge of prosodic forms, a feel for the live and technical fibers of grammar, a familiarity with the syntactic sources of pathos, violence and sublimity, which we can hardly pretend to equal. They may have worked at the surface of language, but it was a surface intricately mapped —and far more literature than romantic theory would have us suppose *is* surface, conventionally impelled and publicly construed. Scholastic and Renaissance grammarians knew that, whatever else he may be, the great writer is a technician, an artisan exhibiting profound but ultimately public, understandable skills. The grammarians of Port Royal in the seventeenth century, who are so much invoked in current debate on transformational grammars, were the direct heirs of this tradition of scholastic rhetoric.

Why the eighteenth century should have been so largely indifferent to the linguistic structures underlying literature is a problem which, to the best of my knowledge, has been little looked into. The reasons are probably far-reaching. The eighteenth-century ideal was, fundamentally, one of lucid paraphrase: the lyric or dramatic genre being an elevation, an embellishment of a content which could, in turn, be extracted from the poem and laid out in everyday

131

prose. Those criteria of intelligibility, robust clarity and ordered sequence which provide the finest of neo-classic and Augustan writing with its distinctive urbane force, were, in the best sense, prosaic. Moreover, that universal civility which the eighteenth century strove for—the notion that almost the entirety of felt and thought life could be articulated in elegant, unobtrusive French—militated against any warier, more penetrative view of the limits or local depths of language. To these factors we must add a characteristic vein, which will run ever broadening through the Victorian and modern periods, of Horatian-Christian moralizing. The work of literature was to be judged not as a linguistic artifact, defining its own stylized, extra-territorial standards of truth and relevance: it was to be seen for its explicit ethical content, and judged accordingly. Dr. Leavis' remark on Samuel Johnson's Shakespeare criticism can stand for an essential trait in the entire Augustan age:

> Not really appreciating the poetry, he cannot appreciate the dramatic organization; more generally, he cannot appreciate the ways in which not only Shakespeare's drama but all works of art *act* their moral judgements. For Johnson a thing is stated, or it isn't there.

Or, to put it otherwise: the eighteenth century values great literature in spite of rather than because of the language in which it conducts what is to us its unique, determining life.

But it was precisely in the late eighteenth century, with Sir William Jones's famous paper on Sanskrit and its relations to Greek and Latin of 1786, that comparative linguistics in the modern sense gets under way. By the 1820's many of what we now recognize as the essential problems in the study of language had been clearly posed.

That August Wilhelm von Schlegel should, at the same time, be a literary critic of major importance, one whose stress on the organic nature of a work of art exercised great influence on the entire romantic movement, and Professor of Sanskrit in Bonn aptly illustrates the new mood. It is from the early nineteenth century on that technical linguistics, the philosophy of language and the study of literature will engage in a joint—though often interrupted and mutually suspicious—collaborative enterprise. And they will do so with an awareness of complexities and a sense of discriminations between possible disciplines very different from the confident classifications of literature and rhetoric made by ancient and medieval grammarians.

In Coleridge almost every aspect of the modern note is struck at once and with a resonance reaching to our own day. I have in mind Chapters xv through xxii of the *Biographia Literaria*, texts in which a poetic and a linguistic sensibility conjoin with a perceptive acuity, breadth of exact inference, and consciousness of the orders of difficulty involved which I would still judge unsurpassed. Coleridge's presiding notion is plain: "For language is the armoury of the human mind; and at once contains the trophies of its past, and the weapons of its future conquests." Crucially, there lies behind this statement a conviction, possibly derived from Kant and Schelling, that language is less a passive mirror than an intensely energized beam of light, shaping, placing, and organizing human experience. We "speak the world," and the poet does so with exceptional reach and steadiness of focus. From this conviction derive the delicacies and re-creative precisions of Coleridge's practical criticism of Shakespeare and Wordsworth. Consider this passage on the effects of meter (Chapter xviii):

As far as metre acts in and for itself, it tends to increase the vivacity and susceptibility both of the general feelings and of the attention. This effect it produces by the continued excitement of surprise, and

133

by the quick reciprocations of curiosity still gratified and still re-excited, which are too slight indeed to be at any one moment objects of distinct consciousness, yet become considerable in their aggregate influence. As a medicated atmosphere, or as wine during animated conversation; they act powerfully, though themselves unnoticed. Where, therefore, correspondent food and appropriate matter are not provided for the attention and feelings thus roused, there must needs be a disappointment felt; like that of leaping in the dark from the last step of a staircase, when we had prepared our muscles for a leap of three or four.

It is not only the manifold incisiveness of the passage that calls for comment and reflection: it is the unobtrusive but undeniable anticipation of those directions of thought which, today, are designated by semantics, the contrastive study of stress, psycho- and even bio-linguistics. Or take the definition—no less rigorous for being itself imaged— of the special excellence of Wordsworth's representations of nature: "Like a green field reflected in a calm and perfectly transparent lake, the image is distinguished from the reality only by its greater softness and lustre." Note, finally, the control of what Coleridge himself termed "speculative instruments," the firmness of critical vocabulary which informs the stricture that there is in some of Wordsworth's poetry "an approximation to what might be called *mental* bombast, as distinguished from verbal."

That the avenues opened by Coleridge's "linguistic poetics" were not followed up during the course of the nineteenth century—some of Baudelaire's critical writings being an exception, though an exception directed most trenchantly toward art rather than literature—is, in part, an accident of the availability or absence of personal genius. There are respects in which Coleridge had no immediate successor but Newman. More emphatically, the two great energies of nineteenth-century literary study were moralistic and historical. The moral tradition leads from Dr. Johnson to Matthew Arnold and ultimately to Leavis. The historical tradition is that of Sainte-Beuve and Taine, whose modern heir would be Edmund Wilson. Comparative linguistics, with its marked successes in establishing the genetics and morphology of Indo-European languages, ran parallel to the understanding of literature. Mutual contacts were few and superficial.

But it is Coleridge's presence which stands most vivid and premonitory when the modern "language revolution" gets under way at the turn of our century.

II

As I have sought to show elsewhere in this set of essays, that revolution had many congruent sources. The re-examination of the foundations of mathematical logic which we associate with Hilbert, Frege, and the early work of Russell led both to the development of modern symbolic logic and to the key recognition that such logic, no less than mathematics itself, was a code, an information structure, with dilemmas and potentialities relevant to the understanding of language. The work of Cassirer on the essentially symbolic nature of human expression (work rooted in Vico and Coleridge) touched at more than one point on that of the symbolic and mathematical logicians. Though initially unaware of the fact, even resistant to it, the psychoanalytic movement was, fundamentally, an exploration of language habits, of the verbal gestures of consciousness; the raw material of the psychoanalytic process is inevitably linguistic. The insights of psychoanalysis into the neuro-physiology of mental life remain conjectural; its disclosures in the realm of linguistic usage and taboo, of semantic ambivalence and pathology are firmly established. Correlative to this movement we may

135

cite the methodical study of the evolution of speech in children as it is found in Piaget.

These several currents of thought were clearly parallel to those at work in philosophy: behind Wittgenstein's proposition that philosophy is essentially "speech therapy," behind the insistence of his *Investigations* that the philosopher's natural and pre-eminent job is the elucidation of men's uses of syntax, lies a far-reaching mutation of attitude. Linguistic philosophy, which has since Carnap, Wittgenstein, and Austin been so dominant in our very sense of the philosophic enterprise, represents a reaction against the confident architectures of total meaning, of total history or metaphysics that mark Hegel, Comte, and the nineteenth century. But it also represents the belief that any true examination of meaning is, first and perhaps also in the final analysis, an examination of the relevant grammar, of the instrumentalities of language by and through which man argues and experiences possible models of reality. This belief and its enactment in philosophy, literature, and art are, I think, directly concordant with a profound crisis of confidence in language brought on by the ruin of classic humanist values after 1914. The investigations of silence, of the limits of language in the face of extreme human need which characterize the work of Wittgenstein, of Kafka, of Rilke, of the Dada movement, which have persisted to the near-silent music of Webern and the voids of stillness in Beckett—these are of a piece. Having become dubious of the powers and humane values of language, logicians, writers, and artists returned to language with a wary consciousness.

It is precisely from this period that we can date that collaborative interaction of linguistics and poetics foreshadowed in medieval rhetoric and in Coleridge.

The main facts are well known. In 1915, a group of students at Moscow University founded the Moscow Linguistic Circle. A year later, a number of young philologists and literary historians started the Petersburg Society for the Study of Poetic Language. From the outset, these associations were characterized by an exceptionally intimate collaboration of poets, technical linguists, and historians of Russian language and literature. At the famous occasion when Roman Jakobson read his paper on "Khlebnikov's Poetic Language"—a paper which foreshadowed almost the whole development of the current linguistic analysis of literature—Mayakovski was present. Poets such as Gumilev and Akhmatova were in close touch with the linguistic analyses of poetic syntax undertaken in Petersburg by Viktor Sklovski and Boris Eichenbaum. With the publication, in 1916, of a joint volume of *Studies in the Theory of Poetic Language*, the modern movement is fully under way. The mere titles of such papers as L. Jakubinski's "The Accumulation of Identical Liquids in Practical and in Poetic Speech" or Eichenbaum's "How Gogol's 'Overcoat' is Made" (with its innovative study of cadence, phrasings, and image clusters in a piece of narrative prose) define a scheme of work which is only now being fully realized. Through his knowledge of Slavonic philology, of poetics, and of the new theories of language being developed by Saussure, Jakobson united in his own work the principal energies of the Formalist or linguistic-poetic approach. His treatise *On Czech Verse*, published in 1923, may be seen as the first instance of a methodical application of modern semantic (or, as they are more technically called, semasiological) criteria to a comparative analysis of the structure and effects of metrical patterns. The choice of language was no accident. With the increasing Marxist attacks on Formalism and Jakobson's own departure from the Soviet Union, the focus of linguistic poetics had shifted to Prague.

Certain Czech scholars would trace the beginnings of the linguistic school of Prague back to 1911; what is certain is that the Prague Linguistic Circle held its first meeting in October, 1926, and that it rapidly became an influential center for the examination of literature in the

137

light of linguistics. The contribution to current linguistic sensibility made by Jakobson, by N. S. Trubetzkoy, by J. Mukarovski, would be difficult to overestimate. It is here that those concepts of structuralism and semiology which are now so fashionable were first set out, and set out with a responsiveness to the genius of poetry and the demands of exact philology which current imitations, particularly in France, often fail to match. It is in the Prague manifesto that concepts which are today banal were first formulated: language is "a coherent whole in which all parts interact upon each other"; "only poetry enables us to experience the act of speech in its totality and reveals to us language not as a ready-made static system but as creative energy"; "everything in the work of art and in its relation to the outside world . . . can be discussed in terms of sign and meaning; in this sense, esthetics can be regarded as a part of the modern science of signs, semasiology." Or, to put it quite simply: the study of a poem is an attempt to register exhaustively the semantic elements or signal-structure of which that poem is made and through which alone it reaches our consciousness.

The Conference on Style held at the University of Indiana in 1958 (like the conference on linguistics and anthropology held at the same place six years earlier) was calculated to summarize forty years of work already accomplished and to map future collaborative progress. It was here that Roman Jakobson summed up what are to be the main effects of the language revolution on our understanding of literature. First, an admonition:

> The poetic resources concealed in the morphological and syntactic structure of language, briefly the poetry of grammar, and its literary product, the grammar of poetry, have been seldom known to critics and mostly disregarded by linguists but skillfully mastered by creative writers.

And then the programmatic statement:

138

All of us here, however, realize that a linguist deaf to the poetic function of language and a literary scholar indifferent to linguistic problems and unconversant with linguistic methods are equally flagrant anachronisms.

How far have these aims and recognitions, first argued in Petersburg and Prague half a century ago, been fulfilled?

Any attempt at a comprehensive answer would, necessarily, become a bibliography. It would have to include an analysis of the special branch of linguistic and poetic practical criticism represented by the instigations of C. K. Ogden and the actual writings of I. A. Richards and William Empson. It would examine the fragmentary but formidably suggestive "hermeneutic" criticism of Walter Benjamin, with its endeavor to combine a linguistic with a sociological methodology in the reading of baroque drama and of Baudelaire. It would want to say a good deal (though, so far as I am concerned, with much adverse caution) of the "semiotics," "semiology," and "structural grammatology" presently flourishing in France. It would invite close attention to a number of key texts: Josephine Miles's "More Semantics of Poetry" (1940), John Crowe Ransom's "Wanted: An Ontological Critic" (1941), Christine Brooke-Rose's *A Grammar of Metaphor* (1958), I. A. Richards' "Poetic Process and Literary Analysis" and Jakobson's "Linguistics and Poetics" (both in 1960), Samuel R. Levin's "Poetry and Grammaticalness" (1964). Professor Stephen Ullmann's studies of the syntax of the French novel would be highly relevant as well as Donald Davie's two incisive books on energy and structure in English verse. One would want to look at the suggestive analyses of coding, information patterns, and narrative structure in primitive or archaic folk songs and oral recitation, made by T. A. Sebeok and Tzvetan Todorov. Already the terrain is very large and impossible to align according to any one single criterion of intent or success.

Nevertheless, the charge that all this deployment of linguistic resources, of philosophic intelligence, of trained sensibility to the poetic life of language, has not really contributed all that much to our reading of a poem cannot be ignored. Time and again, it will be said, the application of sophisticated semantic categories, the quasi-mathematical dismemberment of a literary text, the lexical and syntactic elaboration of its armature produce conclusions that are either unconvincingly esoteric or platitudinous. Surely we had no need of Jakobson or Saussure to tell us that the juxtaposition of Anglo-Saxon with Latinate words in a Shakespearean line makes for dramatic contrast, or that the stressed array of sharp vowel sounds in a poem by Mallarmé—the letter *i*, for example—makes for distinct effects of brittle whiteness and chill. And, above all, what have linguistics, semiology, psycho-linguistics contributed to the root problem of invention, to our understanding of the process whereby certain human beings find words which are profoundly new, yet somehow occasion in the reader of the poem a mystery of immediate recognition?

To plead the exceeding difficulty of the whole business is no evasion. It turns out that a complete formal analysis of even the most rudimentary acts of speech poses almost intractable problems of method and definition. Even the existence or rigorous designation of morphemes as "the smallest individually meaningful elements in the utterances of a language" is not universally accepted, and there have been recent attempts to define the atomic parts of speech in terms even more restrictive or more grammatically active (*i.e.*, the use of the notion of "sememes"). A glance at any current work in transformational generative grammar shows what intricate operations and philosophically or psychologically conjectural presuppositions are enlisted in the normative description of the simplest three- or four-word sentences and phrase-units. Dr. Leavis' admonition, though I regard it as ultimately mistaken or oversimplified, that "language, in the full sense, in the full concrete reality . . . eludes the cognizance of any form of linguistic science" is worth keeping in mind. Indeed, whether there is, as yet, a genuine "linguistic science," as distinct from a body of preliminary hypotheses and partial empirical *données*, is highly arguable.

Transpose these difficulties into what is, unquestionably, the most complex of all semantic phenomena, a poem, a major literary text, and the fantastic complication of the job becomes obvious. Each of the elements of the act of communication which linguistics seeks to define and formalize assumes, in literature, an exponential force and intricacy. In decoding or analyzing formally simple messages, linguistics and semiology come up against obstinate problems of context. How far back must the computer or human recipient read in order to be certain of the right sense of the particular phrase or even single word? In a poem, perhaps even in a work of the length of a novel by Flaubert, the relevant context is total. Every single verbal and syntactic building-block bears on the meaning of any particular passage. Between that passage or line of verse and the entirety of the work, reciprocal qualifications, illuminations, ironic or supporting undercurrents are operative. Our sense of the given phrase or paragraph alters the live shape of the book and is, in turn, transmuted by it. The organic, self-informing nature of a literary text makes formal analysis of single semantic units or moments extremely vulnerable. The same is true of such notions as "tone," "stress," "valuation," "register," each of which is decisive to the significance of any element in the poem.

Yet it is precisely these notions, even where they occur in the most conventional of daily speech forms, that have, until now, defied accurate linguistic classification. That language is polysemic—*i.e.*, that the same word can mean very different things and articulate this diversity simultaneously—has been known since the day when Odysseus

141

used a linguistic pun to rout the Cyclops. In poetry, and in much literary prose, polysemy, with all its devices of word-play, *double entendre*, ambiguity, and phonetic echo, is constant. A great poet is one around whose use of any individual word is gathered a magnetic cluster of resonance, of overtones and undertones. When the Ghost tells Hamlet that the secrets of Purgatory would make his hair stand on end "Like quills upon the fretful porpentine," the phrase strongly suggests an heraldic crest. This suggestion has been prepared for, mutedly, by Horatio's previous description of the Ghost as "Armed at point exactly, cap-a-pe." Now the intimation and associated family of images is developed: the Ghost admonishes Hamlet that the dread truths of Purgatory must not be *blazoned* forth. Originally, *blazon* signified a painted shield; by derivation it comes to signify the act of disclosure, of identification, which is the object of heraldry. But the mere sound of the word, here the echo being simpler and deeper than that of a pun, makes us apprehend the *blaze*, the cleansing fires in which the Ghost is doomed, for a time, to dwell. Shakespeare could not "know" that modern philology ascribes a remote, common origin to the two words. But that knowledge was active and implicit in his total use of all valuations and tonalities of language. Or take the Fool's prophecy in *Lear* that his master shall be treated *kindly* by Regan. Terrible queries and ironies lie in that little word. Is there *kindness* in our human *kind;* what if each man deal after his *kind?* And did Shakespeare, with his ultimate responsiveness to the manifold pointers in language, implicate the common etymological stem which makes of *Kind* the German word for "child"?

How is linguistics, laboring as it does with the "deep structure" analysis of such pronouncements as "John loves Mary," to cope?

Yet a good deal has been achieved, especially in regard to psychological attitude and in regard to an awareness of the orders of difficulty which are involved. Serious readers of literature do read differently since, say, Jakobson and I. A. Richards. The sense of the ways in which a poem defines its own semantic sphere, in which the criteria of significance are internalized, has been sharpened. We deal far more prudently than did either Dr. Johnson or Matthew Arnold with the matter of poetic truth; we act on the supposition that metaphoric language has verifications and consistencies that are internal, and whose justification has a logic, properly speaking, a *symbolic logic* of its own. Our perceptions of the means of syntactic dislocation used in poetry, of the specific determinations generated for the ear by certain phonetic and phonological sequences, are more responsible than those available to nineteenth-century and to impressionistic criticism. An understanding of the combinatorial nature of prosody, of the manner in which the graphic scheme of a line of poetry can either accord or conflict with phonemic patterns, has already produced solid results in the study of sixteenth-century and modern verse. A statistical analysis showing that segmental sound effects in Pope are likely to correspond to lexical meanings whereas in Donne, probably intentionally, sound effects rarely coincide with syntactic and semantic units, is more than ingenuity: it implies fundamental insights about the differences in the use of feeling and expressive means as between Metaphysical and Augustan poetics. The doors opened in 1921 by Sklovski's famous essay on *Tristram Shandy* as a parodistic form of narration, analyzable by precise linguistic tools, will not soon be closed.

Above all, it is our awareness of complication that has deepened. We know, as we did not before, that if literature, of some kind, is a universal phenomenon, if the contrivance of a language-world, related to but also profoundly distinct from that of sensory fact, is general and probably spontaneous to men, the product is special and fiercely difficult to interpret fully. We know a little more than did previous cultures about the anti- or counter-worlds of the poet, and about the intensely circumscribed free-

143

dom within which they operate. We are drawing near, albeit by very small steps, to grasping the scandalous wonder whereby a set of oral or written signals can create characters more "real" and assuredly more lasting than are our own and the lives of their creators. What enigma of the autonomous vitalities of language lies in Flaubert's bitter outcry that he lay dying whilst Mme Bovary, the petty creature of his verbal labors, would endure? In brief: our concepts of literature grow richer and more provisional. T. S. Eliot's celebrated dictum about something "having happened to the mind of England" between the time of Donne and that of Tennyson not only strikes one today as portentously unverifiable: it embodies the style of judgment of what may well prove to have been the last major literary critic almost wholly innocent of a training or interest in modern linguistics.

But, rather than draw a balance-sheet, I should like to list some of the principal problems and possibilities that lie ahead of linguistic poetics.

III

That study of the special linguistic nature of poetry begun with the discussions on *epitheta ornantia* in the Moscow Linguistic Circle fifty years ago, must carry forward. We want to know more about the suspensions of conventional causality and logical sequence in poetic discourse. We want more exact knowledge (the question was already posed by Plato) of the "kinetic" working of different meters and stanzaic patterns, of the ways in which stress, accentuation, rhyme, repetition, assonance, enjambement affect our nervous receptors and trigger emotions often concordant with, but at times directly subversive of, the manifest content of the poem. In the 1930's, I. A. Richards was confident that this "rhetoric of effects" lay within analytic reach; it has in fact proved elusive. We need to know a good deal more than we do about the epistemological tactics whereby a poem (Wallace Stevens' "Anecdote of the Jar" being a great exemplar of this theme) divides itself from reality, yet, if the poet's authority prove sufficient will insinuate into reality new possibilities of order and relation:

> The wilderness rose up to it,
> And sprawled around, no longer wild.
> The jar was round upon the ground
> And tall and of a port in air.
>
> It took dominion everywhere.
> The jar was gray and bare.
> It did not give of bird or bush,
> Like nothing else in Tennessee.

As it happens, a formal, syntactical analysis of the last two lines will encounter difficulties that lead straight to the secret genius of the poem.

Consisting of large units and being, apparently, so diffuse in structure, prose has proved strongly resistant to close analysis. Saintsbury's history of English prose rhythms now impresses one as over-simplified and often doctrinaire. But it is becoming clear that the linguistic elements which go into the creation of a major prose style—say, that of Tacitus, of Swift, of Stendhal—are no less accidental and no less susceptible of formal investigation than are those of verse. The frontier zone, so much exploited since the 1880's, in which prose-poetry and poetic prose meet, is, from a linguistic point of view, particularly revealing. A great prose—Diderot's *Neveu de Rameau*, Kafka's *Metamorphosis*—has a music of its own, and one for which we do not, as yet, have adequate notation.

The typology of literary genres and conventions of style is still at a rudimentary stage. The habits of memory, of narrative unfolding, of formulaic description in an heroic epic reflect a congeries of social, economic, psychological, and linguistic factors. The history of the sonnet, from Petrarch to John Berryman, is the history of a very special, yet perennially formative, contour of statement; a sonnet organizes the world in a way which numerous poets have found indispensable, but whose deep-lying rationale is not yet completely understood. The career of the ode is that of a certain cast of emphatic, public feeling. There are fundamental but obscure interrelations between the rise of the novel and the changes occasioned in men's experience of time by the growth of science and industrial technology. Language anticipates and enacts the altering pulse of material life. In what ways has the *accelerando* of modern communication—the lightning sparsities of telephone and telegraph—militated against those habits of elaboration, of adjectival richness, of verbal ceremony, which underlay verse drama? What correlations can be shown between changes in sexual life and changes both in actual verbal taboos and in the cadence of contemporary prose? In what respect do changes now occurring in our speech habits lead one to anticipate the new and different genres which will follow on the decline of the novel?

We possess scarcely the rudiments of a theory of translation, of any model of how the mind operates when it passes from one language to another. Speaking of the attempt to transfer into English a Chinese philosophic concept, I. A. Richards remarked: "We have here indeed what may very probably be the most complex type of event yet produced in the evolution of the cosmos." But what kind of event is it? Are we dealing, as the Sapir-Whorf hypothesis argues, with a situation in which each of the perhaps four thousand languages now current on the earth articulates a specific, ultimately irreducible segmentation of reality? Are different languages radically diverse modes of structuring and experiencing reality? In which case, even the best of translations is a species of mimetic approximation or illusory transfer. Or are the foundations of all languages a finite set of innate universals—this being the

146

view of Zelig Harris, Chomsky, and transformational grammar? If this is so, the possibility of genuine translation follows, and the deep-structure analogues of human tongues will be found to outweigh the surface disparities. In this domain, the language revolution has crucial bearing. Being a search for underlying patterns of essential significance, the problem of translation has affinities with symbolic logic and the study of language itself as a combinatorial code.

Considerable labor and expense are going into the matter of machine translation. This, in turn, is a special branch of the uses of computers for linguistic analysis. Let me say at once that I am skeptical. I suspect that even the most sophisticated computers furnish models of phrasing which are far too elementary, far too schematic, to throw real light on human linguistic competence and performance. Particularly in regard to determinations of meaning and of implication, judgments that are based on a grasp of the entire relevant context, the ten-to-the-fourteenth-power electro-chemical cells and synapses in the human brain operate at a speed and at a level of selective finesse which, I would suppose, lies totally beyond the reach of mechanical computation. I am skeptical also with respect to the potentialities of machine translation. Here there is widespread confusion. The construction of giant special glossaries is definitely possible. Such glossaries may indeed speed up dramatically the laborious process of the translation of scientific and technological documents. But such electronic glossaries, however refined, are no more than super-dictionaries; they are aids *to* human translation. They do not, in any true sense, translate a body of normal linguistic matter into a parallel body in another language. The summation put forward by Dr. Yngve in the *Proceedings of the American Philosophical Society* in 1964, seems unassailable: "Work in mechanical translation has come up against a semantic barrier. . . . We have come face to face with the realization that we will only have ade-

147

quate mechanical translation when the machine can 'understand' what it is translating and this will be a very difficult task indeed." And so far no evidence has come in to contradict the conclusion of the so-called ALPAC report issued in Washington in 1966: "There is no immediate or predictable prospect of useful machine translation." Nonetheless, the lines of investigation which have led to these negative conclusions are of the greatest linguistic interest. Through them we are learning a great deal about the nature and limits of language, about the concepts—hitherto so largely impressionistic—of what is meant by the possibility or impossibility of literal and of poetic translation. In certain strictly defined areas, moreover, such as the statistical determination of the relations between the literary and the vulgate vocabulary at any given period of history, such as the accurate description of the rates of mutual interpenetration of absorption of different languages, or in the analytic mapping of lexical and grammatical habits in a particular author or body of anonymous work (the Pauline epistles, the "Junius" letters), computers do have a useful role. Indeed, it is exactly at the point where they fail that they may tell us most of the singular genius of language and of the "language animal."

Beyond all these questions, immensely difficult as they are, lie even wider or more intricate queries and possibilities of study. Are certain languages more apt to literature than others? All societies of which we have knowledge devise and perform music. By no means all have a literature, except in the most rudimentary and vaguely expanded sense of the term. Are the primary factors social, economic, geographic? Or is there in the very structure of certain languages a latency of poetic invention? Was there that in ancient Hebrew and Greek grammar which generated or, at least facilitated, lasting forms of symbolic statement, whereas neighboring cultures—Egypt, for example—produced ritual texts but not the free, non-utilitarian play of fiction? Man is a primate who can lie, who can make "impossible" and counter-factual statements. What quality in the fabric of certain languages has transmuted this strange capacity into literature? Are certain tongues more anchored in the material truths of reality than others? What of the poetics and metaphysics of the future tense, that strange resource whereby the human mind pre-empts a tomorrow which the living speaker will not experience and whose very existence is a piece of syntactic inference? Is poetry, in some fundamental sense, always part remembrance and part prophecy—the very reality of past and future being wholly a convention of language? Do certain so-called primitive tongues, whose tense and case systems are far more ramified than those in, say, Greek, French, or English, inhibit the development of literature just because they have affixed to reality too numerous and too precisely divisive a set of labels?

There is the profoundly disturbing question of linguistic entropy. Do great languages "run down," do they lose their speed and accuracy of creative reflex? Do they close windows in their community rather than open them? Is there in languages—Hebrew and Chinese being the only decided exceptions—a life cycle of prodigal growth, confident maturity and gradual decline? Are the critical elements behind the fact that twentieth-century English literature, with the exception of D. H. Lawrence, is so largely the product of American and Irish poets, novelists, playwrights, essayists, economic, political, social, or linguistic? If, as seems likely, all those elements are present, how do they interpenetrate? Does the presence of a Shakespeare (or, analogously, of a Dante, Cervantes, or Goethe) in a language inhibit the development of later resources? To an observer, it is very nearly an unavoidable conclusion that English as it is spoken and written in England today is an enervated, tired version of the language as compared with the almost Elizabethan rapacities and zest of American English and of the breathless literature it is sending into the world. Which is cause, which is effect? Somewhere ahead of us lies a discipline of socio-linguistics, a collaborative inquiry by literary critics, linguists, sociologists, and psychologists, of which we have, as yet, only indistinct premonitions. But the question itself is of the utmost importance: it may well be that cultures and societies die when their uses of language atrophy.

Problematic and, in many ways, scarcely defined as so many of these topics are, I confidently believe that the serious study of literature will have to engage them. This means that the separation between literary and linguistic studies still prevalent in so many universities, must be reviewed. To regard oneself as qualified in the study of literature while being totally ignorant of the changes which modern logic and linguistics have brought to our sense of language is an arrogant absurdity. To write yet another impressionistic or polemically motivated treatise on the virtues of Henry James's prose or the wit of Donne, without grappling with the linguistic facts of the case, is a largely private academic game. Yet, half a century after the Moscow and Prague investigations into language and poetics, such is, among faculties of literature, still the common practice. The reasons are not far to seek. Modern linguistics imposes a certain investment of mental effort. It requires some modest degree of acquaintance with formal logic. It asks of those who think about language seriously that they recognize the relevant neighborhood of that other great idiom of human conjecture which is mathematics (a recognition that has given to such twentieth-century writers as Valéry, Broch, Borges, and Raymond Queneau their distinctive magic). Literary dons, facing classes made up, increasingly, of young women, are not always inclined to refurbish their dwindling stock of obsolete perceptions. But if literary studies are to have a future other than modish, if they are to emerge from an ambience of trivia and personal recrimination such as obtained in theology at the close of the last century, a critical but honest collaboration with linguistics must occur. I do not accept Jakobson's claim that it is "the right and duty of linguistics to direct the investigation of verbal art in all its compass and extent" —*direct* being the overstatement, and literature being far too manifold a phenomenon for the exhaustive control of any linguistics as yet conceivable. But I subscribe fully to the conviction that the student of poetics and the student of linguistics must work closely together if we are to gain further insight into the most decisive and complex of human acts—which is speech, the use and transmission of the *Logos.*

This insight is native to the poet, and it is in poems that make of language itself their theme that we draw nearest the center. Let me, therefore, quote two texts: in the one, language is experienced as harbinger of death, in the other there is a statement of the mystery of its unquenchable life.

Whether a private recitation of a fourteen-line poem on Stalin caused Osip Mandelstam's arrest on May 30, 1934, and led, later, to his deportation and death is not certain. What lies beyond doubt is the concentrated terror of the work. Here is Robert Lowell's very loose adaptation:

We live. We are not sure our land is under us.
Ten feet away, no one hears us.

But wherever there's even a half-conversation,
We remember the Kremlin's mountaineer.

His thick fingers are fat as worms,
His words reliable as ten-pound weights.

His boot tops shine,
His cockroach mustache is laughing.

About him, the great, his thin-necked, drained
    advisors.
He plays with them. He is happy with half-men
    around him.

151

They make touching and funny animal sounds.
He alone talks Russian.

One after another, his sentences hit like
    horseshoes: he
Pounds them out. He always hits the nail, the balls.

After each death, he is like a Georgian tribesman,
Putting a raspberry in his mouth.

It would be fatuous to attempt an exhaustive reading of
this poem, particularly as I am unable to do so in Russian.
Here language is acting at the utmost level of concentration, allusive range and tonality. Everything matters: every
sound, every pause, the unequal lengths of lines (the Russian text is so compact that Lowell's version, economic as it
is, runs to two extra verses). All I want to draw attention
to is the way in which Mandelstam's poem, or, if you will,
sustained epigram—for there are touches that resemble the
art of Martial—images and enacts a notion of language as
being itself murderous.

Such are the enforced silences of Stalinist terror that no
one hears a man's cry for help or intimation of love ten
feet away. Only half-conversation is possible, the ashen
whispering of the damned and of those soon to be shadows.
In a powerful conceit, the poem defines linguistically
Stalin's lunatic omnipotence: *he alone talks Russian*, the
rest of the vast land is silent or makes "funny animal
sounds." In the final dictatorship, only one man can use
the instruments of speech. He does so to castrate and kill,
each word a ten-pound weight. And after language has
killed, Stalin pops in his mouth the blood-red and musky
flesh of the raspberry. This is a poem about the limits of
language, about the decline of men into abject, comic ani-
mality when speech is denied them. But, being itself so
eminent an act of language, Mandelstam's fable defines
the suicidal privilege and necessary job of the writer in the
communities of the inhuman.

Because it must savage that in man which is most humane—namely, the gift of language—barbarism has often sought out the poet. The eleventh book of Ovid's *Metamorphoses* (and Mandelstam, like Ovid, wrote a *Tristia*) tells of the slaying and dismemberment of Orpheus. Arthur Golding's version of 1565–7 is, of course, the one Shakespeare knew. It tells how "heady ryot out of frame all reason now did dash, / And frantik outrage reigned." Of how the crazed maenads

> ran uppon the prophet who among them singing stands.
> They flockt about him like as when a sort of bird have found
> An Owle a day tymes in a tod: and hem him in full round,
> As when a Stag by hungrye hownds is in a morning found,
> The which forestall him round about and pull him to the ground. . . .
> And (wicked wights) they murthred him, who never till that howre
> Did utter woordes in vaine, nor sing without effectuall powre.
> And through that mouth of his (oh lord) which even the stones had heard,
> And unto which the witlesse beastes had often given regard,
> His ghost then breathing intoo aire, departed. . . .

All nature mourns the death of the singer who made the forest fall silent. The nymphs descend the mourning rivers "in boats with sable sayle." But *mirum!*—wonder:

> dum labitur amne,
> flebile nescio quid queritur lyra, flebile lingua
> murmurat exanimis, respondent flebile ripae.

> His head and harp both cam
> To *Hebrus* and (a wondrous thing) as downe the streame they swam,

His harp did yeeld a moorning sound: his liveless
    toong did make
A certeine lamentable noyse as though it still yit
    spake,
And bothe the banks in moorning wyse made answer
    too the same.

In death, his body rent, the poet sings still.

Let this serve as metaphor—as is Orpheus' descent into
Hades—for the singular power of language to bring and
to overcome death. In Mandelstam's poem, words are the
literal killers of the poet. In Ovid's narration of Orpheus,
language is seen to endure, like a live flame, in the mouth
of the dead singer. It is the business of the student of literature and of the linguist to listen closely, to explore, so far
as we may, the exercise of creation which is speech. Reader,
critic, linguist are *answerable* to the poet—in the full meaning of that word which contains both response and responsibility. There lies our common bond, and the fascination
of the job ahead.

IN A POST-CULTURE

In *Mes Pensées*, which were probably set down during the 1730's or '40's, Montesquieu remarked that the ancients had been "living books." They had *known* history, whereas the moderns *owned* history: *"C'est la découverte de l'imprimerie qui a changé cela: autrefois on estimait les hommes; à présent, les livres."* Mallarmé's famous letter to Verlaine, with its vision of the *Grand Oeuvre*, of the supreme book, *"Le Livre . . . tenté à son insu par quiconque a écrit,"* is dated November, 1885. Very roughly, the century and a half between the two dicta defines the classical age of the book, the time in which books, as material facts, as moral concepts,[1] mark a principal focus of the energies of civilization. A specific fabric of economic and social circumstance, a specific set of ideological conventions and reflexes of feeling, made that focus effective.

The classic act of reading takes place in a context of privacy and leisure. Eighteenth-century engravings or paintings of *La Liseuse* emphasize the elegance, the privileged apartness of the pursuit. Reading demanded a surrounding yet private spaciousness, as did chamber music. It also needed a degree of silence, and with the growth of urban, industrial society, silence is a measurable luxury.

[1] This is one of the points at which McLuhan's argument most obviously needs modification. The central authority of the "print culture" develops much later than Gutenberg and has had a short history.

Both the production and the consumption of books in the classic sense presuppose fiscal, domestic, almost architectural modes which are characteristic first of the *ancien régime* and next of the high bourgeois structures of the nineteenth century.[2]

Le Livre depends also on a shared referential literacy. The sources of that literacy were, of course, Greco-Latin and Hellenistic-Christian. They are assumed and vital in the means of literature from, say, Caxton to *Sweeney Among the Nightingales*. Both the text and the reader's response are organized by firm habits of schooled recognition. A pact of common awareness has been negotiated, as it were, before book and reader meet. The author has at his disposal an indispensable shorthand of allusion: to Scripture and the classics, to preceding literature, to a large but well-defined idiom of historical and philosophic inference. He takes for granted a *consensual* reflex, more or less exactly informed but, in any event, rapid, whereby his reader will know of the nightingales, of that bloody wood in which they sang, and of Agamemnon crying loud. He assumes also a ready apprehension of traditional communicative means, such as analogy, metaphor, trope, rhetorical indirection. His book enters on a field of prepared echo.

This resonance effect is again a phenomenon with particular social and economic foundations. The level of vocabulary, of grammatical control implicit in the classic exercise of reading, is, very nearly by definition, an élite acquirement, inseparable from certain privileged standards of education and verbal usage. But the consensus of echo on which the authority and effectiveness of books depended went deeper than schooling. A corpus of agreed

[2] It is true that certain exceptional works, such as *Pilgrim's Progress*, were read under conditions of "mass consumption." But they are few and far between, and their characteristic strength seems to derive from earlier, oral sources. It was Dickens' peculiar genius to enlist these archaic responses while, at the same time, being a master of middle-class book-culture.

reference is in fact a set of philosophic, social values. The economy of statement that makes possible a literary style, and the recognizable challenges to that style by the individual writer, have underlying them a large sum of undeclared but previously agreed-to social and psychological presumptions. This is especially so of the high literacy between the times of Montesquieu and of Mallarmé. The kind of lettered public they had in view is directly expressive of an agreed social fabric. Both the linguistic means and range of matter of books—in short, the semantic whole of authorship and reading—embodied and helped perpetuate the hierarchic power relations of Western society.

They also embodied a deep trust in language, in the capacity of language to inform—in both, crucial, senses of the word. That trust was founded on a long, intricate history. It drew on the Hellenistic identification of word and spirit and on the trope, as forceful in post-Cartesian rhetoric as it had been in the Neo-Platonism of the Renaissance, that clear, eloquent discourse constituted the preeminent singularity and excellence of man. Literate speech and, perforce, writing was the guarantor of civilization, the dynamic inventory of its cumulative riches and available capital. But it was more than a repository: the literate code, by virtue of plainly understood omission, served to exclude, to ostracize into silence or into the zone of taboo expression, large areas of indecorous or frankly menacing psychological and social fact. Much of reality did not exist or led a half-life of conventional, obscuring hearsay simply because there was no acceptable language in which to express and experience it.[3] A Molière or a Swift could ridicule the confines of tolerable statement and even enlarge them to include sexual and social material previously inadmissible. But because it was itself carried out within classic expressive modes, their subversion was, to use cur-

[3] We need a serious investigation of the social, historically specific coördinates of "word-blindness." Societies, as well as individuals, can develop "reading-blocks" as a defensive or suppressive mechanism.

157

rent jargon, quickly "encapsulated." Where it occurs within agreed lines of social force, laughter need not admit new reality—it can disarm it.

The trust in language stemmed from and also made active the great convention of *mimesis*, the assumption of a representative interrelation between language and the facts of the world. No doubt that relationship was subject to alteration and even crisis. It was ancient doctrine or, at least, metaphor that pre-lapsarian speech had been immediate to the truth, that the tongues of fallen men related to reality only as through a glass darkly. Jurists of the sixteenth century knew that words had changed their meanings, sometimes in bewildering ways. Nevertheless, the speech and writing of sane men were profoundly congruent with the grain of things. Set down with sufficient care and observant of the long-established logic of syntax, words would constitute a true mirror of the world and of its history. The *Encyclopédie* is the chief monument of that mimetic confidence. But it was manifest as well in every "serious book" and in the conviction that the act of reading was one of importation from certified reality—of importation made possible by the stability and agreed value of linguistic coin.[4]

This whole enabling structure is now much eroded.

The decline of privacy, of its caste and space co-ordinates, has been drastic. The guarded aloneness—guarded both by domestic service and by sheer floor or ceiling room —that defines the traditional private library is now rare.

[4] The topic of the relations between fiscal and linguistic currents is one of the most difficult in the theory of culture. The interpenetration of sexual and monetary fields of reference has been established by psychoanalysis. So, to a more conjectural extent, has been the relation of these fields to the larger area of semantics and symbolic coding. What is needed now are specific, localized studies of the possible correlates between attitudes toward speech and toward money (such categories as hoarding, waste, scarcity, devaluation, conspicuous consumption, would appear to apply to both "currencies"). Are there, for example, verifiable analogies and instrumental links between the excess of liquidity, the long trend to inflation in recent American economic history, and the contemporaneous plethora and devaluation of linguistic means?

The density of silence in which the classic exercise of reading took place (consider the changes in the noise levels of the night city) is today anomalous. Moreover, contrary ideals have come forward. Images of collective, festive, openly communicative "togetherness" are dominant. The act of silent reading is, unquestionably, solipsistic. The man who reads without moving his lips, a performance first recorded by St. Augustine, is shutting out others. For most people, assuredly for those who are not expert enough to follow a score, listening to music is simultaneously a more passive and a more social business. It matches, far better than does silent reading, our current ideals of participatory leisure.

Mass education and the liberal dogma of general access to culture have largely undermined the trained consensus of traditional literacy. That consensus may, indeed, have been a matter of caste complicity, but, far more then hitherto, we are now beginning to gauge the degree to which a high civilization and its values are conspiratorial in form and preservation. With the conspiracy, as it were, unmasked, the old fabric of agreed recognitions is no longer natural. So much of Western literature is "about" previous literature; so much of it is an unfolding reiteration, by means of allusion and variant, on an established repertoire of motifs. Today the knowledge needed for unforced response is rapidly becoming specialized, academic knowledge. The glossary and footnotes lengthen on the page, bending the text out of immediate shape, interposing a strangeness between its direct address and the reader. The idiom of Shakespeare and Milton, and, what matters more, the habits of recognized verbal form and classical reference from which that idiom derives much of its central motion, are passing out of reach. Soon even the most rudimentary of shorthand markers—from classical mythology, from theology, from history or philosophy—will have to be explained, and will take on a false, learned tonality. Ask a "common reader" to make unaided sense of Milton's

159

Lycidas or of one of Keats's odes. But the new pastoralism, with its distant roots in romantic anti-intellectualism, is not only unresponsive to the referential texture of a good part of literature. That "impulse from a vernal wood" is set against "book-learning" as a whole, in a dialectic which substitutes a myth of immediate experience for one of, presumably, derivative, second-hand response.[5]

Populist and mass technocracies are characterized by a semi-literacy. By a widely disseminated ability to read simple texts, and a corresponding inability to penetrate syntax to any but the shallowest reach (recent estimates put the literacy of more than one half of the adult population of the United States at the level of twelve-year-olds). Such semi- or sub-literacy is not being eradicated by mass schooling: it is being made politically and psychologically acceptable. So far as Western culture is concerned, sub-literacy is probably the major difficulty. But one ought not to forget the profoundly disturbing increase of actual illiteracy on the world scale. The latest UNESCO estimate puts at almost half of the world total that number of primary-school children who drop out before attaining literacy. In Latin America, the proportion often reaches seventy-five percent.

Symmetric to sub-literacy is the decline in the authority and comprehensiveness of language itself—as the term "language" is used and understood in a formal culture. To regard worry about the current condition and future vitality of language as "modish" is simply to fail to see what is involved. With the splintering of knowledge and the fantastic proliferation of specialized sub-languages, the literal

---

[5] The present cult of "immediacy," the demand that each human being "do his thing" with complete vehemence of personal being, is, in fact, a reverse élitism. The number of individuals who have a fresh, life-enhancing "thing to do" is, at any given time and level of society, highly restricted. For most persons, the derivativeness of experience in a classic culture meant an equal measure of participation in riches of feeling decidedly greater than those which ordinary sensibilities can discover for themselves. The demand (so emphatic in D. H. Lawrence and his libertarian heirs) that each erotic experience be "orgasmic" and creative is a precisely parallel piece of blackmail against common resources.

compass of educated discourse has shrunk. The use of mass media of communication by political and mercantile interests—both equally totalitarian in their claims against privacy and individual choice—has immensely intensified those processes of falsification and dehumanization which have always been part of the uneasy relations between language and the state.[6] Investigations of this crisis were begun by Fritz Mauthner and Karl Kraus. The "failure of the word" is a primary theme in modern literature, from Lichtenberg and Kafka to Paul Celan and Beckett. Awareness of this complex, pervasive phenomenon ought to be a commonplace. All I would emphasize is the obvious bearing of the language crisis on the traditional centrality and stability of the book.

The last, perhaps most important area of erosion is more difficult to get hold of. I have in mind a widely perceptible, but awkward-to-define, transformation in the status, in the conceptual focus and attendant mythology, of personal identity and of death. This is much too large a topic even to state rigorously in a short paper. But it has crucial relevance to the notion of *le Livre*. Underlying most of serious literature from the jubilant close of Pindar's Third Pythian Ode to Eluard's *dur désir de durer*, and underlying a coherent response to that literature, is a gamble on transcendence. The writer intends the words of his poem, the imagined personae of his drama or novel, to outlast his own life, to take on the mystery of autonomous being. So far as he allows the text a new life within his own consciousness, the reader collaborates with that intent. The trope of "immortality" together with the vital echo of recreative reading constitutes a classic culture. But we no longer invoke "immortality" in that sense, or, if we do, it is with a tinge of archaicism and ironic solemnity. The notion, almost axiomatic in classic art and thought, of sacrificing present existence or content to the marginal chance

<hr>

[6] I have tried to argue these issues in detail in *Language and Silence* (1967).

of future literary or intellectual renown seems to grate on modern nerves. To most younger people, it would seem hypocritical bathos and a subtle perpetuation of élitist idols.

We see something of this mutation in the sociology of the happening, in aleatory music and "rearrange" sculpture, with their correlative emphasis on what is unique and what is ephemeral. We see it in the aesthetic of the collective and/or anonymous work, in the refusal to stamp a single "great name" on an act of creation. The audience/reader is not merely a loyal echo to the artist's genius, but a joint creator in a conglomerate of free-wheeling, immanent energy. Away with masters.

Certain aspects of this suspicion of transcendence are graphically present in the paperback book. The private library, with its leather spines and shadows, is all but obsolete; the hard-cover tome, the work in more than one volume, the collected *œuvre*, may soon become so. The paperback revolution has obvious economic and sociological sources, related to ever increasing printing costs and the image of a new mass audience (an image which, I think, already needs rechecking). But it also corresponds to deeper internal changes in the status of literacy. The paperback is designedly ephemeral; it does not make for a library in the old sense. The book, as Montesquieu and Mallarmé understood it, had a stability of format to which the current paperback lays no claim. The threefold matrix of literary creation, of reading, and of time defeated or transcended found its expressive guise in the bound printed work privately held, hedged with quiet. Today, the pact with and against time, with and against the authority of the individual ego, operative in the classic act of writing and reading, is wholly under review.

II

It is these changes one must reckon with when asking about new genres. They are so intricate and far-reaching that most of what one can say will be guesswork. The question itself has an obsolete ring. The concept and terminology of genres are very distinctly a part of the classic framework. They may belong to formalities and cohesions of precisely the kind which is now in doubt. At best, one's notes toward the future are bound to be local.

Whether any poetry has ever had a large audience—except under brief and special circumstances—is a moot point. The number of serious poems, excepting the very particular case of the Psalms, that have signified much to anyone beyond a very restricted minority is certainly small. The proposition that poetry is in some ways the highest of human accomplishments, the one most imitative of the original enigma of creation, is almost universally accepted. But that universality is conventional; it is an abstract password of culture rather than something which most human beings have felt in their bones. Via citation, paraphrase, and common reference, the poetic monuments of a high culture lead an immensely diffuse, though unbroken life. But, again, that life is often conventional and culturally coded rather than direct. To how many general readers in the relevant language communities are the *Commedia*, *Paradise Lost* or *Faust* II a privately met, as distinct from a conventionally referential, experience? The question would have had point even during the period of disciplined caste and bourgeois literacy. Today, it is hardly worth asking.

At the moment, two main currents can be made out. The one leads toward verse of deepening privacy, experimentation, and hermeticism. Difficulty serves, since Mallarmé, as a trenchant defense against the Philistine. It keeps out the vulgate and forms an elective aristocracy of understanding. But the hermetic or *intimist* tradition does more than "purify the words of the tribe." It puts the whole of language to the question; it racks and splinters the worn common forms to discover whether there are antique, hidden springs of inventive vision below the frozen crust. Hence

163

the curious violence, the disruptive, scarcely covert hysteria of a good deal of modern experimental poetry, from Mallarmé himself and Stefan George to Dada and Celan. There is also a strain of autism in such poetry. Language is focused on language, as in a circle of mirrors, and by modulation the principal subject or organizing myth of the poetic enterprise is poetry itself. Again, the force used can be violent, but it remains implosive. It is not meant to reach outward.

The second main current, on the contrary, is public, dramatically external, and often collaborative. It has its obvious inspiration in Whitman and Pound. It is the voice of the megaphone and the read-in. In both America and Russia, vatic, declamatory verse is reaching large audiences. In both societies, there is at present an absence or decline of traditional cultural modes and an intense hunger for the politics of promise. Where lies or censorship prevails, poetry can be news in the literal sense. Above all, as is so clearly seen in the work of Voznesenski, of Yevtushenko, of Neruda, the poem is a conspiracy in the open air. The counterworlds of language, the rhetoric of fantastication, are a critique—probably the only critique that can be made aloud—of political reality. Where they are involved with drugs, the public-histrionic modes reach back to the private. At times now, we get poetry which is simultaneously oratorical and hermetic as none had been since Rimbaud.[7]

In as much as semi-literacy and political oppression will continue to characterize much of organized society, both the esoteric and the public currents of poetry will persist. Between them, presumably, there can be many types of experimentation and lyric circus: "do it yourself" poetry, possibly related to the use of computers; concrete poetry and the use of poetic texts, perhaps randomized or subject to constant reticulation, on large walls and public spaces.

[7] The "amphitheater-kabbalism" of Allen Ginsberg is a representative example.

But it is difficult to think of any of these graphic and mechanistic variants as genuinely radical. There is little in current devices which is absent from the aesthetic of Schwitters and Duchamp. The radical genius of Dada and of Surrealism is far from being exhausted; theirs is, still, the tradition of the new. I have heard of only one poetic mode that seems entirely original. A sometime student at the Royal College of Art in London chose a precise point in space—the halfway marker on a Dutch dyke—and a precise instant in time—say, half past four on a specific afternoon. Having defined these unique, unrecapturable co-ordinates, he arranged for another human being, a friend, to meet him at the exact given intersection of these arrows of time and place. He termed this meeting a work of art, a totally controlled modification of reality, involving the deviser and the respondent in a collaborative creation. There is something at once haunting and absurd to the project: a sense of the poem as the creation of a total setting, as the momentary imposition of arbitrary order on inchoate possibility.

The situation of the novel is a stale topic. Ninety percent of prose fiction is read as casually and quickly as it is remaindered. Today, a "great novel" is a form whose inferred strength and logic are almost deliberately archaic: witness Solzhenitsyn's *The First Circle*. The novel embodies the linguistic conventions, the psychology, the habits of sensibility, the code of erotic and economic power relations, of precisely that middle-class civilization which is now passing.[8] The classic novel is both a supreme achievement and a normative element of that civilization. Like many of the institutions and formal presences which it articulates, the novel will have a considerable afterlife; a

[8] The profusion of "high" pornography, produced and championed by serious novelists, particularly in France, during the past two decades is suggestive of a rear-guard or nostalgic action. It is as if the prose novel, conscious of its rapid decline, was attempting to "catch up" on an area of feeling and narrative experiment which it had been forced to leave to one side in its classic period.

165

nostalgic or parodistic animation may continue. But the vitality of expressive need is largely gone. The numerous appeals now being made to the genius of George Eliot and Tolstoy, the inference that we need only return to these great exemplars to get things right again, are precisely analogous to those made throughout the late seventeenth, the eighteenth and the nineteenth centuries to the epic lineage of Homer, Virgil, and Milton. It took centuries for poets to realize that the high verse epic was a form gone inert, a genre whose social, stylistic, metaphysical presuppositions could not be artificially revived.

What we see at present is the powerful diffusion of fictional techniques into non- and part-fiction. The inventiveness, the stylistic energy, the eye for scenario and symbolic detail which abound in current biography, history, political record, and writings about science are directly inherited from the novel. If so much non-fiction is better written than current novels, if it is far more adult and crowded with felt life, the reason is that the major period of the novel has come before. It is his acute awareness of these polarities and his virtuosity in the intermediary phase which make of Norman Mailer the representative case. Where fiction is purest, where it crystallizes the ancient impulse toward mythical narration, it is also very brief and extraterritorial to all those normal furnishings of daily life which are the specific strength and substance of the classic novel. I have in mind the *Fictions* of Borges—who has said recently that the short tale will have more staying power than the novel—or the parables of Beckett.

It is difficult, and probably spurious, to discriminate formally between "drama" and the great spectrum of live representational genres which include radio, television, cinema, the happening, the be-in. There are good reasons for supposing that a post-culture will find these forms indispensable to its imaginative coherence. A society with few private libraries and a sharply diminishing readership (a survey conducted in 1969 concludes that the *per capita* consumption of books in France is of the order of one per year) can be a society of numerous screens, arenas, and playhouses. Much is being said just now of a return to oral modes. The concept is obviously suggestive. But a distinction must be made. Ancient oral-aural techniques were *explicitly conservative;* their aims were those of exact remembrance and transmission. The audio-visual means of the mass media are calculated toward maximal impact and instant obsolescence. The difference is fundamental. Even to the extent that they can be seen or heard more than once, the radio play, the film, the television show constitute a strictly immanent, essentially ephemeral act. Their relation to time and to the dynamic echo of reiteration in later consciousness is radically different from that of the book. Why it should be that even the best of films becomes intolerably stale and static after a third or fourth viewing is a complex question. There is, after all, a sense in which the printed text of a great poem or novel is equally fixed and can be regarded as equally *déjà vu.* But, whatever the reason, the fact remains.

The theater appears to be yawing uneasily between a past ideal of literary stability and the new lines of total freedom and event. There are regards in which Brecht's *Werke*, with their theoretic apparatus, are closer to Ben Jonson's *Works*, with their aspiration to monumentality and lastingness, than is either to Peter Handke's *Sprechstücke* and Beckett's *Act Without Words*. In the current welter of meta-forms, and at a point when new technical devices such as the audio-visual cassette may alter the whole definition of what is public and private spectacle, of what can be stored and of what is one-time-only, it would be foolhardy to augur. Two points may be worth making. A look at the post-war film, at television drama and television features, at the radio play, shows a formidable investment of creative talent. The reserves of imagination at any given period in a society are finite. Previously, a large proportion of that talent would have gone into literature and drama.

The thinness of the novel could relate directly to this drain. Undoubtedly, the genius of film and of the best of television are shaping a literacy of their own. But the allocation of a substantial part of the visionary energies of a society to the production of significant ephemera is, at least in the West, a new and problematic phenomenon.[9] The other point bears on the concept of "play." Playing and the play, *das Spiel* and *das Theaterspiel*, are interacting vividly. Scene and structured environment, or environment experienced as dramatic setting, are drawing close. Politics (notable violence) as agreed ritual, action in the streets modulating into acting, the new or the derelict landscape as deliberate backdrop—these are notions that occur readily as one thinks about the future of mimetic and participatory forms. But I do not know how they will mesh and just how the *game* will make a *play*.

It is more profitable to point to some of the books which are truly exploratory, in which the old forms can be seen fragmented and the new foreshadowed. Some years ago, I suggested the name "Pythagorean genre," meaning simply that there have been since, say, 1900 a number of books in which the energies in motion of music, the presence of mathematical and spatial symbolism, of language as magic, have liberated or made secret traditional forms of discourse. The philosophy of lyric, dramatic address in Kierkegaard and Nietzsche—the direct miming, the enacting of abstract argument—has exercised a subterranean but ever more powerful influence on a whole range of linguistic forms. It will take time before the revolutionary structure of Ernst Bloch's *Das Prinzip Hoffnung*, which is part epic voyage, part imaginary memoir, part ontological treatise, and language experiment throughout, will have been grasped, let

[9] I make a reservation because there is in non-Western culture a long history of the production of complex, highly inventive artifacts in materials intended for almost immediate consumption or destruction. The dominant trope of Western literate culture calls for the creation of poetic and plastic forms "that shall outlast bronze and break the tooth of time."

alone exploited. Kierkegaard may, again, be the root of the use of the essay as lyric and hermetic form. Some of the "essays" (the word is roughly approximative) of Walter Benjamin, or Carlo Emilio Gadda's *Ero e Priapo* with its virtuosity of invocation, incantation, flyting, philosophic masque, are among the most inventive shapes in modern literature. We are seeing also a new hybrid of private, nearly occult vision with a body of public, pragmatic discipline: in Lévi-Strauss's *Tristes Tropiques*, in John Cage's extraordinary *Silence*, with its links, perhaps, to Mallarmé's *Un Coup de Dés*. There are the combinations, so suggestive of other potential orderings, of poetry, feuilleton, drama in Karl Kraus's *Letzten Tage der Menschheit*, in David Jones's *Anathemata*. Péguy's rejection of the logic of linear statement in *Victor-Marie, Comte Hugo* was prophetic. All these are radical acts, new and contemporaneous with Blake.

Because high culture, in the classic sense, is now becoming obsolete, there have emerged parodistic genres of "surrealist scholarship," fantastications of knowledge in which learning that was once part of schooled sensibility is taking on a grotesque and distant air. The four-volume translation and exegetic commentary produced by Nabokov "at the occasion of"—there is no exact rubric available—Pushkin's *Eugene Onegin* is one of the comic-nostalgic masterpieces of the age. Even the index is parodistic. Or consider the uses of bibliography, of formal logic, of philology in Borges' fables. It may be, as Thomas Mann seems to have implied in the end of *Felix Krull*, that it is only via ironic fantasy that traditional learning and the new world of the sciences will enter into the general currency of language and metaphor. This is, to me, perhaps the most exciting frontier: the "translation" of the world-image of the sciences into common speech, into general feeling, by means of lyric, parodistic, tragi-comic projection. Raymond Queneau is a key figure in this regard: witness the comic mathematics of *Bords*. Already there are vital permeations between

169

the exact sciences and deeply imaginative statement. I would put forward, with every seriousness, the proposition that the work now in progress that comes nearest to the sustained re-creative design of Proust, which comes closest to rivaling Proust in its "re-experienced structuring" of an entire past and society, is Joseph Needham's *Science and Civilisation in China*. Proust on the altering focus of the steeple at Martinville and Needham on man's realization, across centuries and cultures, of the true shape of the snow crystal are exactly comparable exercises in total imaginative penetration. In each, there is an intense poetry of thought, readily felt but extremely difficult to paraphrase.

What these different genres and radical forms have in common is the act of writing, *l'écriture*. It is *l'écriture* in itself, rather than the books it produces, which now engages critical debate, particularly in France, and in the hermeneutic tradition that is developing in Germany, Italy, and the United States in the wake of Heidegger and Hans-Georg Gadamer.[10] What are the relations of the act of writing to other types of action, in what ways does *l'écriture* limit or falsify the ontological freedom of language, what are the relations between the writer and the individual psyche—his own, the reader's—in the social and semantic ensemble? In what way must the new art of reading, as Heidegger would have it, be a "hearing of that which is not in the lines"? The vivacity, the sheer critical intelligence with which such questions are being posed is undoubtedly a gain. Much of the inertness of the current state of English criticism and literary study can be gauged from its indifference to these centers of argument. But that vivacity is, also, in a sense, spurious. It marks an unmistakable Byzantinism and malaise. There has been an acute loss of nerve in the face of the old confident injustices and ex-

---

[10] Some of the key texts are Heidegger's *Unterwegs zur Sprache* (1959); H.-G. Gadamer: *Wahrheit und Methode* (1960); Paul Ricoeur: *De l'interprétation* (1965). Richard E. Palmer's *Hermeneutics* (1969) offers a good general introduction to this wide field of linguistic and semantic philosophy.

clusiveness of a high culture, in the face of the old trust in the representative truth of language. What will survive (the archaic question) of the present, often brilliant assemblage of writing about writing? Is there, at some covert level, a strain of barbarism, of profound disillusion with literacy, in the jargon with which current neo-scholiasts pursue their inquest? At the grave of Henry James, Auden asked intercession for the vanity of the writer's calling, for the treason of all clerks. Vanity and treason there were; Mallarmé's image of the universe as *le Livre* is a capital case. But there was also the hope of creating against time, of making language outlast death. That is the essence of a classic literacy. Not very many, today, admit to the arrogance, to the obsessive aloneness needed for that hope.

171

LIFE-LINES

A scientific revolution is an act of motion. The mind leaves one major door of perception, one high window, and turns to another. The landscape is seen in a fresh perspective, under different lights and shadows, in new contours and foreshortenings. Features that were salient now appear to be secondary or are recognized as elements in a more comprehensive form. Details hitherto unobserved or casually grouped assume a dominant focus. The grid of the world alters, as it does when it is seen from an incoming plane as it banks over a lit city. It is rare for such realignment to be brought on by a single discovery or by a single discipline, though one might argue that this is just what happened when celestial mechanics altered the geography of the mind in the seventeenth century. Usually, a scientific revolution gathers impetus over a wide field. At roughly the same time, singularities, obstinate anomalies in different sciences become, as it were, magnetic. Oddities that have been classed tentatively, or circumvented in the confident ordering of the main lines, begin moving toward the center. (Small irregularities in the mechanics of corpuscular motion and of the propagation of light instigated the new vision of relativity physics.) Attention is drawn to what had been marginal, perhaps professionally suspect phenomena. The investigator tinkers with the accepted model. He has been educated inside it;

it has given a framework to his own research. His science enters a glue-and-pieces-of-string phase; a crack is filled here, a strut mended there. During this stage of *ad hoc* carpentry, eminent work can still be achieved. Even after Copernicus, the Ptolemaic scheme, corrected, modified, stretched at the awkward corners, continued to produce superb observational astronomy. But there comes a time when the job of repair grows too costly. Kepler has to abandon the ancient, intuitively satisfying conviction that planets move in regular circles.[1]

The stubborn eccentricities in the old model now loom large. The cracks widen and afford glimpses of a very different perspective. In the manner of iron filings when the magnet moves, numerous details, local perceptions, heretical conjectures, theorems stumbled across but discarded in more confident moments gather to form new patterns, new fields of meaning. Reconsidered, the ancient anecdotal detail—medieval pilgrims finding seashells and fossil ferns near mountaintops, or an old parlor trick such as white light being fractured into a rainbow through a prism—becomes a crucial aspect of a new manner of seeing the evolution of the earth or the laws of optics. Most significantly, the shapes of science itself, the relations of inclusiveness and of method between the sciences, change. Specialized branches become the main trunk, areas formerly at the heart of the pattern are seen to be inert or minor offshoots. After Descartes, geometry—once the queen of exact sciences—becomes largely a localized topic of algebra. Not much of classical chemistry is now active: physical chemistry, molecular biology, the investigation of atomic particles have subsumed the raw material of chemistry, and the questions it once asked, under new

---

[1] Cf. Thomas S. Kuhn: *The Structure of Scientific Revolutions* (1962). More detailed and psychologically penetrating material, though argued from a somewhat different point of view, may be found in Alexandre Koyré's *La Révolution astronomique* (1961); *Newtonian Studies* (1965); *Etudes galiléennes* (1966); *Etudes d'histoire de la pensée scientifique* (1966).

mappings. Astronomy as it was understood in the eighteenth and nineteenth centuries is a local case of astrophysics. One need only look at the lives of Fermi, Oppenheimer, Wolfgang Pauli to remember that as late as the 1920's atomic physics was a bizarre field for a young scientist to choose and one that a number of the most creative physicists chose only because traditional, established academic sciences were difficult to break into, on social and ethnic grounds.

Scientific revolutions—there have not been many in Western history—show certain characteristic symptoms. The old framework is not wholly scrapped. Only in regard to Mercury have substantive changes been made in the beautifully accurate plottings of planetary motion achieved by Ptolemaic astronomers. The foundations of Euclidean geometry have, since the mid-nineteenth century, been seen to be a special case—a point of view among several of equal validity and formal reach. But we continue to order almost the entirety of our lives and cognitions as if space were indeed a three-dimensional construct of plane geometry. Ideally, the new horizon incorporates the old. This is not always possible. Modern psychopathology cannot comfortably house the old theory of "humors," and our present understanding of gases and chemical bonds will not accord with the once powerful notion of phlogiston. But more often than not the principal data and techniques of the previous model fit into the hierarchy of the new. They are seen to have been in some sense a special or preliminary statement of a more comprehensive, more dynamically flexible synthesis. The second distinctive trait of a full-scale revolution is the shift to a new center. Renaissance ballistics were much concerned with the mathematics of weight and directed flight. With Galileo and Newton, this sub-topic moved into the very heart not only of the natural sciences but of man's consciousness of ordered intellect. The study of hysteria and aphasia had subsisted on the "melodramatic fringe" of classic mentalism; after

Charcot and Freud, it became the pivot of a new working image of the human person.[2]

The other identifying mark of a first-order scientific revolution is the emergence—indeed, the proliferation—of new and intermediate disciplines. The altered landscape shows new contiguities, new traverses between key territories, new stream junctions and deltas. A classic unity splinters—into chemical physics, physical chemistry, molecular biology, biogenetics, biophysics. Radio astronomy, X-ray astronomy, astrophysics emerge from the ancient node of philosophic cosmology and celestial mechanics. Already there is a "geology of the Moon," or selenology, and already there are perfectly coherent plans for a paleontology of the planets. A modern crystallographer works amid the debris and conjunctions of half a dozen obsolete or regrouped disciplines.[3]

Finally, a revolution in and of the sciences will escalate outward, to have an impact on sensibility, on the general climate of civilization. The effect may be more or less rapid. The Copernican-Galilean revolution was slow to penetrate lay consciousness; even the celebrated quarrel between Galilean astronomy and the Aristotelian orthodoxy of the Church was a specialized, esoteric affair. The impact of Newton, on the other hand, seems to have been rapid and wide-ranging. Via high gossip and literary metaphor, the world picture of the *Opticks* and the *Principia* became fashionable. We can speak of a post-Newtonian mode in prose and poetry, in social argument, in the general style of educated feeling. Something analogous followed on the confirmation of Einstein's predictions of the curvature of

[2] Cf. Michel Foucault: *Histoire de la folie à l'âge classique* (1961) for the background to this change.

[3] Comprising, as it does, so many and diverse aspects of speculation—alchemical, mathematical, mineralogical, molecular—the history of the sciences of crystals and crystallographic structures is a privileged compendium of successive scientific and intellectual movements. There are, currently, several mathematical and observational fields in which the theory of lattices, ultimately derived from a study of crystals, is at the forefront.

light passing through the gravitational field of the sun. A "relativistic" vocabulary spread across the arts, philosophy, and even certain schools of music. The actual content of the new science may not be accessible to common insight (it certainly was not in the case of relativity physics). As it reaches further into the world of the layman, the particular revolution in biology or physics will tend to be more and more blurred by metaphor, rough analogy, and plain misunderstanding. Even Voltaire simplified or misconstrued a good deal of what Newton was in fact saying. But the great transformation is felt nevertheless. A boulder-strewn New England field does look different since Louis Agassiz; the color of our children's eyes has new meaning—and beauty is a part of meaning—since Gregor Mendel.

II

The scientific revolution that emerged in the late 1950's, and in which we are now involved, seems to have all the marks of first magnitude. It may lead to the most decided transformations of feeling and world-picture since the Galilean and Cartesian models of reality, which so largely created our modern world. The new mappings now in progress are obviously grounded in the great accomplishments of electromagnetic theory, of the physics of wave and particle, of Darwinism and of neurophysiology as it developed from Claude Bernard on. The formidable scientific successes of the later nineteenth and early twentieth centuries, with their deterministic emphasis and linear forms, are not being repudiated. They are being regrouped, lit from a different angle, connected to new mains. But the center *is* shifting. The current state of particle and high-energy physics is a complicated topic. In a sense, theoretical physics is once again in a pre-Copernican phase. A multitude of discrete observations is being organized in various conjectural designs of immense complexity and some strangeness. A unifying insight into the fundamental fabric of matter seems tantalizingly near. But so far it has not been achieved, and there are grounds— related to problems of high-energy generation and to the fantastically small scale on which sub-atomic phenomena occur—for supposing that the confident expectations of the 1950's may be disappointed.[4] Putting the argument with great caution, it seems reasonable to say that the primacy of mathematical physics as the science of sciences, as the exemplary core of general scientific progress, which it has been since the seventeenth century, is now passing.

The new hub is that of the life sciences, of the lines of inquiry that lead outward from biology, molecular chemistry, biochemistry, biogenetics, and ethology in its largest sense. These lines now seem to radiate and spiral toward every quarter of scientific and philosophic pursuit, as did the algebraic physics of Descartes and Newton.

Another trait of a major change is also evident. New and "relational" disciplines are proliferating. Biochemistry and biophysics are themselves in course of fission. Virology, immunology, the several branches of crystallography, the chemistry of enzymes are being drawn into new configurations and proximities. They are interacting within the larger hierarchy of genetics and the molecular biology of life processes. Most significantly, these re-groupings are drawing upon and at some points actually triggering certain branches of mathematics. Topology, the theory of measures, the algebra of lattices are meeting and also directing the new, exceedingly sophisticated demands of

---

[4] The whole problem is of an order of technical and theoretic difficulty such that the layman has very little access to it. But the "retrieval" of phenomena occurring at the scale of 10^{-17em}, the need to interpret such phenomena via immensely magnified representations, seem to pose severe philosophic as well as empirical obstacles. What kind of "reality" is being "looked" at? Conceivably, we are in a phase of limits to observation on both the macrocosmic and microcosmic scale: galaxies whose nearness to the speed of light puts them "over the edge" of the observable field, and particles too small, too short-lived, to be studied in any confident sense.

the biological sciences. One of the key figures in this change is the French mathematician René Thom, who is working on the multidimensional "spaces" in which processes of genetic coding and transmission take place. In short, the "life-science revolution" of the twentieth century will have its distinctive mathematical arsenal as did the physics-mechanics revolution of Galileo and Newton.[5]

Lastly, we are experiencing just now a symptomatic diffusion of new scientific concepts into general literacy. As the sciences become ever more abstruse and mathematical, such diffusion is bound to be mainly metaphoric and imagistic. It is real, nevertheless. It is not only the double helix of DNA that has entered the repertoire of common reference. A history of idiom and simile over recent years would register how markedly such concepts as "information," "coding," "life system," and "environment" have filtered through from specialized, mathematically formalized usage into the speech of everyday. The fact that Newtonian physics found expression in the poetry of Pope, whereas the current scientific changes are being imaginatively echoed mainly in science fiction, does not mean that their impact is less great. It points only to the present vulnerable condition of literature.

To define a revolution of such scope and intricacy in what may only be its early stages is difficult even for the best-placed of scientists. It is nearly impossible for the layman. All he can do is to try to sense the shapes of change, the alterations in the direction and intensity of light as it falls on the scene. Inevitably, he will get things wrong.[6] He will seize on the dramatic episode and miss the central drift. But similar difficulties prevail when we try

[5] Nothing is more instructive with regard to the changing shapes and mappings in Western culture than the ways in which mathematical abstractions move into and out of relation to the applied sciences. Cf. the admirable treatment of the theme in S. Bochner: *The Role of Mathematics in the Rise of Science* (1966).

[6] So, of course, may the scientist. Rutherford's judgment as to the purely academic, esoteric future of atomic energy is a famous case in point.

to grasp—to organize within our own, personal field of reference—a revolutionary movement in the arts, in music, in thought. And the scientists are saying that it is to some of these same movements that their own new vision relates.

It is the critical notations, the crucial counters that are changing. The Galilean scheme of point, line, and trajectory, the straight-line co-ordinates and plotted curves of Cartesian algebra and trigonometry were more than instruments of formal statement. They provided modern science and technology with a graphic logic, with a linear, causal bone structure of hitherto unrivaled resilience and predictive force. Today, it is the "field," the "manifold," the "vibratory amplitude" of phenomena that are being stressed. The contours of vision of classic and even of Einsteinian physics, however abstruse and mathematically "imaginary," were hard-edged. Today, our sense of dynamic processes is beginning to focus on the unstable shell, on the membrane whose functions now appear to be as much a matter of permeability, active transmission, and metamorphosis as they are of separation and distinct identity. In part, the new module arises from the well-known adjustments in the statistical and predictive criteria of particle physics that are called the "principle of uncertainty" or "indeterminacy." The "center" cannot—is not meant—"to hold," and one need only read the fascinating correspondence between Einstein and Max Born to realize how deeply Einstein, who remained an essentially classical physicist, feared the intimations of Yeats's "mere anarchy is loosed upon the world."

But more is involved than the observational limits of indeterminacy. The observer himself, the act of cognition, are increasingly enmeshed in the observed fact. We grow less confident than were Newton or Laplace that "the facts" have a stable eternity "outside" the contaminating range of our altering, culturally, and linguistically governed psyche. To observe is to alter; to define and to understand, even in the most neutral, abstract fashion, is to incorporate the

179

evidence within a particular matrix of human choices, images, and symbolic reflexes. Not since the sixteenth century has scientific and philosophic thought been as conscious of the woven texture of experience, of the multitudinous skeins and cross-weave of relations whereby human consciousness, language, and the phenomenology of the "real world" are close-bound. In an elusive way, by innate analogies that one cannot fully account for, salient changes in art have mirrored those in science. Mondriaan is probably the last of the great Cartesians. The shifting manifolds and provisional spaces of Klee, the dynamic fields and "flow-charts" of Pollock, Rothko's pulsing light are not only metaphors of what is happening in the logic of the sciences. They, too, draw the observer inward, into the active, unstable locus of energy. In *Beyond Appearance*, C. H. Waddington, the eminent geneticist, has looked at these mirrorings of modern art and science.

The scientific world-picture of post-Newtonian physics, of thermodynamics, of old-style biology was characterized by assumptions, often so well-worn as to be unconscious, of linearity, of uniform causal logic, of determinacy. If a process could be viewed "mechanically"—that is to say, in the light of a blueprint with a firm mathematical basis— all the better. It was, to put matters crudely, the inadequacy of this mechanistic ideal to account for major areas of biological and psychological fact—at a time when this ideal was being challenged and modified in physics itself—that brought on the great shift to the life sciences. To put it another way, where the natural sciences have, since Galileo and Kepler, been largely concerned with the transmission of *force* (gravitational, electromagnetic, thermal), we appear to be moving toward a model in which it is the transmission of *information* that matters most. It is the sense of the life processes as realizations of the storage, coding, retrieval, transmission of information that is now in the forefront. Thus the striking encounters of vocabulary— even allowing that they are metaphoric approximations—

between linguistics and biogenetics. Thus the conviction in both domains that the radical wonder of live matter is not mechanical force but *meaning*.

Again, there are far echoes of the Renaissance and sixteenth-century integral view, of the Orphic belief that the grammars and creative modes of human speech have their counterpart in all nature. There is a haunting if deceptive modernity in the notion, so often celebrated by baroque poets and thinkers, that arteries and the branches of trees, the dancing motions of the microcosm and the solemn measure of the spheres, the markings on the back of the tortoise and the veined patterns on rocks are all ciphers.[7] To the symposium of psychologists, neuro-psychiatrists, zoologists, and neuro-biologists who gathered at Alpbach in the summer of 1968, as it was to Francis Bacon and to Giordano Bruno, life is language, and organic processes are articulate forms.

III

Alpbach is a handsome village in the Tyrol. It is also the summer home of Arthur Koestler, who since the 1950's has been concerned with the philosophic and social aspects of the life sciences. Himself a great writer with strong scientific interests, Koestler has been exploring the mind-body problem from two related viewpoints. He has been studying the process of creation, of the genesis of new forms in biology, in art, and in the history of scientific discovery. At the same time, he has been grappling with the question of the nature of human freedom and moral responsibility within the context of seemingly deterministic

---

[7] The history of these analogical structures and, by inference, of their bearing on current sensibility may be found in Elizabeth Sewell: *The Orphic Voice* (1960) and *The Human Metaphor* (1964), and in Frances Yates: *Giordano Bruno and the Hermetic Tradition* (1964), *The Art of Memory* (1966), and *Theatre of the World* (1969).

181

chemical and neuro-physiological theories of the mind. In the course of this work, he has felt deepening discontent with the analytic tools and mechanistic presumptions that the biological sciences had taken over, more or less un-argued, from nineteenth-century physics. The Alpbach Symposium and the proceedings, published in *Beyond Reductionism* (1970), are the result of this malaise. Edited by Koestler and by Professor J. R. Smythies, of the University of Edinburgh, these papers and informal dis-cussions make for a profoundly interesting and controver-sial statement of the new vision.

Koestler's own essay is a useful place to start. He is intent on breaking out of the circle of reductionism, by which he means the use of "nothing-but" definitions. Life is *nothing but* a set of chemical reactions. Behavior is *nothing but* a case of stimulus response. The brain is *nothing but* a computer, or holograph, with a large storage capacity. This way of thinking, argues Koestler, and the "bits-and-pieces" image of the world that it entails violate the true nature of organisms. A living form is more than the sum of its parts—not in any mystical sense, but because the many-leveled, stratified arrangements or hierarchies of parts within parts constitute a dynamic whole. Laid out on the table, the gears and ratchets of the watch are not a working instrument, and—what is, intuitively and intel-lectually, more important—they are not a just model or picture of a working timepiece.[8] But the "dynamic whole," says Koestler, is itself only a bit of shorthand: "Wholes and parts in this absolute sense do not exist anywhere, either in the domain of living organisms or of social organi-zations. What we find are intermediary structures on a series of levels in ascending order of complexity, each of

---

[8] Koestler's point is shrewd but, philosophically, rather shallow. The congruence of *any* model or graphic representation with *any* whole object can be faulted. All models are necessarily static or reductive. Is Koestler confusing the primarily didactic, simplifica-tory function of models with an understanding—which may be complex and vital—of that which they represent?

which has two faces looking in opposite directions: the face turned toward the lower levels is that of an autonomous whole, the one turned upward that of a dependent part." Each of these levels will have its own laws of organization and its intrinsic patterns. By remembering the dynamic status of these "holons"—at one moment the node from which other branches spring, at another the bough that leads to the main trunk—the scientist will overcome the atomistic fallacy—the erroneous image of complex units as mere composites of small, divisible parts. He will understand why complex organisms or psychological and social structures cannot be taken to pieces and put together again, as in a taxidermist's shop.

This does *not* mean—Koestler is emphatic—that the application of analytic techniques and detailed examination of components should be abandoned. It is legitimate to analyze mental phenomena, for instance, in terms of brain physiology, and to approach the immensely complex fabric of the brain via its cellular, molecular, and sub-atomic constituents. But, urges Koestler, we must be clear about exactly what it is we are doing. Each of our analyses will apply only to a fragmentary, specific aspect or parameter of the phenomenon. By isolating it for study, we produce a kind of necessary fiction. Each sub-assembly derives meaning only from its place in the complete hierarchy. It is the lines of communication between hierarchic levels that constitute life. Or, to say it another way, a systematically organized whole cannot be "reduced" to its elementary parts; it can only be "dissected" into its constituent branches. And, however useful, such dissection will produce an ambiguous result: we acquire partial, perhaps novel, information but lose something of the organizing vital pattern. The magnifying glass will show the grain of the canvas; only when we step a good distance back will the thinking eye, by a process of scarcely understood intuitive selection, reconstitute the picture as a significant whole.

Professor Paul Weiss, of the Rockefeller University, gives, in his contribution to *Beyond Reductionism*, an eloquent statement of the vitalist, or "integralist," case. To him, as to the Neo-Platonists of the Renaissance, the universe presents itself "as an immense cohesive continuum." [9] Analytic dissection "can yield no complete explanation of the behavior of even the most elementary living system." Such a system incorporates an irreducible duality of predetermined organization and of freedom. The component activities have many degrees of freedom, of potential spontaneity and innovation. But they submit to the ordering restraints exercised upon them by the integral activity of the whole. There is a constant feed-back process whereby "parts" and "whole" interact. The hierarchy is open to ascendant and descendant energies. In a living system, the structure of the whole determines the operations of the parts; in a machine, the operation of the parts determines a pre-set outcome. Organisms are doubtless made up of molecules, but they "are not just heaps of molecules." At present, says Weiss, it is not clear that we can go much further. The achievements of molecular biology and of neuro-physiology are momentous. "However, we still do not have any inkling of how these fragmentary items of information, obtained analytically, could be combined into a faithful image of the unitary and orderly behavior of our central nervous system, of which we are privately conscious, and the expressions of which we can observe in the overt behavior of others." All we can guess is that the capacity of living things to alter while retaining their identity seems to depend on an almost inconceivably delicate interplay between indeterminacy in the small and determinacy in the gross.

[9] This, precisely, may mark the line of division between a Newtonian and a pre- or post-Newtonian map of reality. Newtonian physics came to terms, though rather uneasily, with emptiness and interaction over empty spaces. The notion of a "cohesive continuum" and the emotional bias it represents points back to the assumptions of Renaissance and sixteenth-century natural philosophy.

184

The dynamics of the "whole" are not, of course, limited to internal processes. Again, in a way which no "taking-to-bits" analysis can show, living matter is a structure of constant interaction between hereditary or endogenous factors and environmental influences. It is virtually impossible to draw a sharp line of demarcation between the innate and the acquired—the more so because of the "presence between the two of the all-important zone of self-regulations." This is how the great experimental psychologist Jean Piaget and his colleague Bärbel Inhelder describe in the symposium the level of self-adjustment or equilibration through which an organism adapts its hereditary potential to the demands and opportunities of the environment. The ability to self-regulate is innate, but the specific modes of adjustment are not. What is unchanging is the capacity for change. In a remarkably wide-ranging paper, Piaget and Inhelder apply this concept to the acquisition of fundamental logical, relational, spatial insights by very young children. Theirs is a plea against behaviorism. The child's action transforms reality at the same time that he is also triggered or transformed by it. The organism imposes a *schema* on the surrounding world. As it develops, as its relations to the environment become more intricate and creative, that *schema* is modified. Thus the fascinating hypothesis that our memory code, far from being fixed and essentially automatic (as is that of a computer), is itself in a constant process of restructuring. We "repack" the past for our new needs as we travel ahead.

The heart of the anti-reductionist case is Professor Waddington's paper on "The Theory of Evolution Today." The problem of evolution crystallizes the attitudes and methods of the present scientific revolution. It does so not only because evolution signifies meaningful change and the transmission of the fantastically complicated life code but because it embodies, at its most evident, the unique faculty of living matter to replicate and yet to change in interaction with the environment. If we can think of a gravitational-algebraic focus for the world picture of much of the natural sciences from Newton to Maxwell, we ought to think now of an evolutionary fulcrum. And it is exactly at the "interface" between that Darwinian-Mendelian theory of random mutation plus natural selection and the recent discoveries in genetics and biochemistry that one finds some of the most characteristic, speculative arguments in current science.

Waddington's presentation is tough going. It draws on fairly recondite aspects of information theory and on the kind of statistics and topology that can handle an organism, such as man, carrying up to a million genes. "Now if we consider each gene as an instruction, and think of the number of ways these instructions can be combined with one another and interact with the surroundings, the possible number of combinations is truly astronomical. If one wants to make a diagram of the situation, one cannot really do it on a blackboard of two dimensions, but topologists nowadays have made us get used to thinking in terms of spaces with an almost or quite infinite number of dimensions." Intuition, together with certain very abstruse mathematical models, suggest to Waddington that this immense number of possible genetic combinations in fact makes for "homeorhesis." This is a coinage, and we may hear a good deal about it in the years ahead. It means a kind of dynamic stability, a "stable course of change" profoundly distinctive of living systems. The first problem is one that in a more rudimentary form perplexed Darwin: why does the whole system not come to an equilibrium, what keeps life evolving? [10] The answer might lie in that zone of creative self-regulation I have mentioned before. As soon as any organism evolves, it will change the en-

[10] Historical distance allows one to suppose that a good many instances of Darwin's notorious caution, of his hesitation before rigorous logical consequences, were based on profound intellectual scruples. It is these scruples, and not Victorian moralism, that influenced and attenuated his analyses. Peremptory Darwinism is, largely, the work of T. H. Huxley, whose *Darwiniana* of 1893 is a characteristic example.

vironments of all other organisms with which it interacts. Life bends and alters the space that surrounds it. If the living system is to exploit these new environments, there have to be mechanisms to disperse organisms sufficiently and mechanisms to produce new variations with a hereditary potential. The first condition offers little difficulty. It is the second that must be brought into accord with recent work on the genetic code and on the reiteration or replication of the genes that code for RNA.

Professor Waddington's suggestions are not easy to paraphrase simply. He argues that it is the function of random mutation not to throw up just the one gene needed for evolutionary adaptation but, rather, to replenish the stores of variation already contained in the population. He seeks, in a most interesting way, to introduce the idea of a "very generalized form of learning" into the fundamental mechanics of evolution.[11] Certain genes may be concerned with the capacity to respond to stress. If the given stress is often met, these genes will be kept in being by the natural selective advantage they confer. Continuing over the generations, the concentration of these genes in the organism will actually modify the otherwise stabilized evolutionary course and produce an altered phenotype (which means simply a type determined by visible characteristics). That is, living forms create their environment and are in turn re-created by it—not in the Lamarckian sense of a direct influence of the environment on the genetic constitution but, rather, by long-continued selection of appropriate responses. It is not the response itself that is inherited but the capacity to respond to the environmental stresses in the appropriate way. "Thus genetic assimilation makes it possible for evolution to exploit what one might call the cleverness of physiological reactions to stressful situations." Discomfort is the spur of life.

[11] This line of argument accords well with very recent experimental work on "learning processes" in monocellular organisms. The difficulty arises when one seeks to discriminate between such processes and mere tropisms.

This scheme, which, as other participants in the Alpbach symposium point out, has some provocative analogies with current theories on the generation of language, hardly answers all questions.[12] The notion that the gene pool is changing while the species remains essentially the same bristles with difficulties. Experimental work seems to show enormous differences in the reiterated DNA of organisms which are otherwise closely related. What sort of selection process can possibly account for the drastic shuffling around of the genetic material that takes place in a few cell generations? We do not know. What is impressive is the point made by Koestler: "It is sheer nonsense to say that evolution is 'nothing but' random mutation plus natural selection. That means to confuse the simple trigger with the infinitely complex mechanism on which it acts."

The name of Lamarck turns up a number of times in the new "vitalist" or "organicist" argument. As Koestler himself observes, Waddington's theory *looks* like a Lamarckian process, though one that is brought about by Darwinian means. Waddington puts forward, cautiously, the thought that the structure of proteins is to some extent modifiable and that "the structure of DNA is not quite so inflexible as we now think." How else is one to account for the notoriously difficult case of the rapid, specific formation of antibodies that resist the introduction of new substances into the organism? None of this means Lamarckianism in the old, primitive sense of the immediate inheritance of acquired characters and of characters implanted by the direct impact of the environment. Lysenko's uncomely ghost is still at rest. But it does mean that thinking about the interactions of hereditary material and the environment—certainly at the level of the individual cell—is far more

[12] I point to such analogies elsewhere in this book. The question is made difficult by the fact that there are in the generative-transformational theory of language aspects which are both innovative and deterministic. In its stress on adaptive freedom, the Chomskian model is "vitalist." In its postulate of innate universals and rule structures, it is often reductionist.

complex and cautious than it was in the heyday of neo-
Darwinian orthodoxy.

I V

To the Sherardian Professor of Botany and Regius Professor of Biology at Oxford, such interactions are the prime
stuff of history. Professor C. D. Darlington's *The Evolution
of Man and Society* (1970) is nothing less than a world history in terms of biological principles. Human history is a
special instance, though undoubtedly the best-documented,
of the interrelations of organic inheritance and changing
environment. The military records, institutional chronicles,
biographies, and social-economic surveys of which nearly
all history books are made up are, as it were, the surface
structures of the underlying, incomparably more important
and exciting course of biological and biosocial evolution.
C. D. Darlington is unquestionably one of the world's
ranking plant biologists and cytologists. His interest in the
evolution and interplay of genetic systems dates back to the
early 1930's. *Genetics and Man* (1964) extended the argument to human affairs. Like the pioneering Russian
plant geneticist N. I. Vavilov, Darlington is one of the
prime movers in the branch of social history that deals
with the relations of cultivation and culture. Any book by
Darlington commands attention, the more so because the
Keeper of the Botanic Gardens of the University (another
of his ancient titles) writes with an exhilarating clarity,
with a power of organization and turn of phrase that put
many so-called professional writers to shame. The result is
a tome of formidable scale and zest that challenges comparison with H. G. Wells. Darlington's panoptic record
goes from the origins of man to the most recent crises of
renewal and fragmentation in Africa and in China. Though
nearly the whole of world history is looked at, there is a
heavy stress on the classical and Western lineage. There

189

is little question in Darlington's view but that Greco-Roman and West European civilization has been the chosen ground of social and intellectual genius. If "the last three thousand years have produced more evolution than the previous twenty million," it is in the tradition of mental adventure which leads from the pre-Socratics and Isaiah to the world of Marx and of Einstein that this extreme *accelerando* can best be traced. In this vast discourse, America and China earn only one chapter each, and the discussion of the whole of Chinese history seems shorter than the erudite review of the culture of ancient Egypt.

Darlington's criteria are firmly based on Mendelian genetics. With inbreeding, heredity is all-powerful and the human group becomes an invariable caste of the type illustrated by Sparta. Outbreeding produces unpredictable variability and the chance of endless innovation. Every human species seems adapted to preserve some kind of balance between these two poles. Failures of adaptation lead to historical crises and to the disappearance of societies. The evolutionary advance in human intelligence varies between races and peoples because the breeding balance deviates by a greater or lesser extent from the ideal. Rarely do we get on the scale of an entire nation or community the equilibrium achieved by the Rothschild family, for example, in which half of fifty-eight marriages by descendants of the founder were between first cousins and half were between unrelated couples.

The principal creative mechanism of history is the coming together of different races to form stratified societies. Societies made of governing classes and of slave classes will always compete favorably against unstratified bodies. (The analogy with current thought on the hierarchy of organic systems is obvious and striking.) Stratified societies —Egypt, Greece, Rome, feudal and eighteenth-century Europe—"were more competent because their genetically different classes coöperated to give a more complex, more efficient product than any primitive homogenous societies.

They were also more adaptable because hybridization between classes could, and in the event of social change always did, release new variability in the stratified society." The most successful of governing élites, be they Aryan, Chinese, or Bantu, have hybridized with their subjects but at the same time, as a caste, kept away from them. Again, the formula is one of finely judged balance. A governing class alone cannot exercise sole power over breeding behavior, for it will inbreed and disintegrate. There is need of a priesthood, perhaps recruited in the dominant caste but also independent from it, to organize a religion whose rules and myths lead to the right practices of cross-breeding. Darlington considers the Mosaic code one of the most enduring solutions to this difficult problem.[13] The lesson is plain: intelligent hybridization is the necessary condition of human progress. The loss of any community, however primitive, cuts down on the potential of genetic encounter and diversity. This, if one will, is the "liberal" aspect of Darlington's case. The other aspect is no less clear: the best circumstances for hybridization are those that prevail in strongly stratified societies and in societies in which individual behavior is subject to the pressures of traditional authority.

Pursuing these guidelines, Darlington recounts the history of Neolithic man, of Sumer, of ancient Egypt and Israel. He deals with the fragmentation of the Greek city-states and the process of empire from Alexander to Augustus. He traces the "genealogy," in the true sense of the term, of Christianity, Islam, and Hinduism. He tells of the unique ferment of energy that brought reformation and revolution to Europe and caused the white races to dominate and instruct so much of the earth.[14] He concludes

[13] The idea that normative codes of behavior, based on religious and ethical authority, are in fact disguised systems of biological regulation is not, of course, new. At this point, Darlington's argument is contiguous with that of Freud and of Lévi-Strauss. The incest taboo is, in each of these theories of history, the focal point at which biological and cultural energies meet.

[14] Current hysteria and masochism regarding the role of the

191

with a magisterial analysis of the interrelations of biological and social man.

This great traverse of time and the map abounds with arresting, often recondite touches. We learn that Charles Darwin never realized that fertilization was accomplished by a single sperm—a failing he shared with the headmen of Indian hill tribes. The understanding of words is ancient, but we have no evidence for any understanding of numbers among Paleolithic peoples. It is because Pope Felix IV begot children that the Church had Gregory the Great. Muhammad committed two grave errors in natural science: by adopting a lunar year, he threw the festivals out of kilter and ruined the Mecca trade fairs forever; by forbidding the men of Medina to pollinate their female date palms, he ruined the harvest. The Kadars in Kerala are "perhaps the only human tribe which can hunt by scent." Stalin's fatal mischief lay in his ignorance of the biological fact whereby a revolution is successful only when it is followed by hybridization with its opponents and not by their extirpation. The extinction of dynasties such as the Ptolemies came about not because of incest—uncle-niece marriages and brother-sister unions were equally fruitful—but because of the unfortunate occurrence that the legitimate progeny were more often murdered than the illegitimate. The Barca family, which produced Hannibal, and the Buonaparte clan both had connections with Majorca. And who but Professor Darlington would affirm that Christendom has been permanently deflected away from crowded southern climes "by its neglect of cleanliness, its opposition to nudity and washing"?

Caucasian minority in the creation and dissemination of human civilization make it nearly impossible to study the phenomenon of "white predominance." Are the roots of that predominance accidental, sociological, climatic, nutritional (i.e., the differing levels of protein consumption)? Those who publicize the outrage of their radical conscience over the "crimes committed by the white man against other races" hardly pause to notice that even their "remorse" —histrionic and opportunistic as it may be—is a phenomenon peculiar to Western sensibility. All races have oppressed. How many have come forward in penitence?

In brief: an immensely stimulating and comprehensive world history, beautifully written. Yet, *on its own terms*, a serious disappointment. All his use of flow-charts and dynastic genealogies does not make of Darlington's book a true "biological history." When the tide of ordinary historical records is interrupted by genetic statements, these are almost invariably extremely generalized. We are told of the "genetic cleavage between nations," of the "gene-flow" between conqueror and conquered, of the universal principle that there can be no equal fusion of "unequal races, genetically and ecologically contrasted races." Precise analyses are not infrequently naïve: Charles I and Louis XVI were both "virtuously wedded to a foreign wife and deprived of advice from any native mistress." Whence their unfortunate destinies. At other points—and they are often crucial—Darlington's statements are, at best, unproven.

How does he know that among Mongolians not one gene has mutated in twenty thousand years? What possible proof has he that the Phoenicians were "real individuals" who did not respect divisions of language and of religion? Precisely what is meant by the statement that the Jews who returned to Israel had a genetic continuity "which stored their wrongs in a collective memory"? In what verifiable way does the observation, fascinating in itself, that the Etruscan lion statue at Vulci recalls a Hittite relief almost a thousand years older authorize the pronouncement that "the genetic continuity overrides the cultural discontinuity"? [15] Does the observation, again fascinating, that Lenin's four grandparents were of four races and religions really contribute much to our understanding of the Bolshevik revolution? Can it be shown that the "intellectual leaders of the Christians of all later times" are in fact the result of the genetic assimilation of newly converted Jews into

[15] I am neither inclined nor qualified to say that Professor Darlington is in error on these points. But he is surprisingly indifferent to the question of what would in fact constitute verifiable proof for his propositions.

the Hellenistic community? Or take the matter of language. Darlington's formula is striking: "Is it through human language that the heredity of the races becomes the environment of the individual." And I believe he is right when he stresses the profound differences between languages and between the related evolution of thought patterns. But when he says that "every people has a genetically different sound-producing apparatus from every other" Darlington is going entirely beyond and probably against the available evidence. All too often the proofs offered for key statements are no better than they were in Carleton S. Coon's disputed *The History of Man* (1954) and *The Living Races of Man* (1965).

This is not so much a criticism of Professor Darlington, whose erudition and range of expert passions must make one diffident, as it is of his enterprise. Even in a present-day community, under rigorous observational conditions, the determination of genetic facts and possible social correlates is exceedingly precarious. When we deal with the distant past, and with phenomena on a continental or millenary scale, the documentation is simply unavailable. Looked at closely, a good number of Darlington's clinching arguments are arrived at after the fact: a positive, brilliant historical or cultural development is proof of successful hybridization. Failure, in turn, shows genetic crisis. The demonstration can be turned on its head with dangerous ease.

The point can, perhaps, be made most simply by contrasting *The Evolution of Man and Society* with *History of Bubonic Plague in the British Isles* (1970). Professor J. F. D. Shrewsbury's monograph is almost as long as Darlington's *summa*. It deals with a single though very important point of interaction between biology and society. It is masterly in its scruple, in its analysis of the acute difficulties of judgment that arise even where evidence is precise and extensive. Seeing Shrewsbury grapple with the question of whether it is possible to assess the social, genetic impact of the Black Death in a single county, one comes to wonder at the assertive sweep of Darlington's conclusions.

Both the Alpbach symposium and Darlington's history have been vehemently attacked. A large number, perhaps a majority, of orthodox and experimental biologists have seen in Koestler's "holons" and Waddington's "chreods" animist fantasms not much different from the oracular vapors of Teilhard de Chardin. The "Koestler clique" has been assailed for abandoning those very ideals of empirical verification and analytic determinism to which the natural sciences owe their prodigious advance. Recent progress in the laboratory reconstruction of the complex molecular chains of enzymes seems to represent precisely the approach that the Alpbach vitalists are rejecting. C. D. Darlington, in turn, has been denounced as a racist. This charge cannot, I think, be sustained. But damaging critiques have been made both of his Spenglerian generalities and of specific details in his argument.

Yet in the case of both books, the sharpness of controversy points unmistakably to the importance of what is being said. Working outward from highly technical issues in genetics, biology, biochemistry, linguistics, Darlington and the scientists who met with Koestler have put forward suggestions that touch on almost every facet of human history and social conduct. Theirs is precisely that centrality of concern which so little of current philosophy and literature succeeds in communicating. I have no doubt that theories of "coding" and of "fields" will soon be prevalent in the study of art, of music, of social institutions. Already the biological disciplines, linguistics, and anthropology are working in close mutual awareness and with an often shared vocabulary. This is a revolution of perspective that concerns us all. The biogenetic and biosocial investigations now under way touch directly on the shape of our lives, on the beliefs we profess, on what expectations we may have of the survival of a sickened culture. The anti-reductionism

195

of Alpbach may be no more than a polemic salvo in the early stages of a scientific revolution. Darlington calls his vast treatise "merely a sketch which raises more questions than it settles." Once raised, however, such questions will not rest.

The prospects are exhilarating but not without menace. Since the Renaissance, Western civilization has operated on the confident assumption that the needs of man, that the requirements of social justice and personal worth, would prove to be in more or less natural accord with the discoveries of science. There might well be awkward patches, such as those caused by the excessive spread and pressure of industrial technology. But, all in all, man and the truth were companions. Certain trends in the life sciences now cast doubt on this assumption. It is as if the biochemical and biogenetic facts and potentialities we are now beginning to elucidate were waiting in ambush for man. It may prove to be that the dilemmas and possibilities of action they will pose are outside morality and beyond the ordering grasp of the human intellect. We seem to be standing in Bluebeard's castle. For the first time, the forward-vaulting intelligence of our species, which is so intricate yet so vulnerable a piece of systematic evolution, finds itself in front of doors it might be best to leave unopened. On pain of life.

INDEX

GEORGE STEINER

Born in Paris in 1929, George Steiner is now Extraordinary Fellow of Churchill College, Cambridge. He commutes often to the United States, where he has been Albert Schweitzer Visiting Professor in the Humanities at New York University, and where he has taught also at Stanford, Princeton, Harvard and Yale. After taking degrees at the University of Chicago and Harvard, where he won the Bell Prize in American Literature, Mr. Steiner was a Rhodes Scholar at Oxford. He served on the editorial staff of the *Economist* in London from 1952 to 1956. At that time he became a member of the Institute for Advanced Study in Princeton. There he wrote *Tolstoy or Dostoevsky* and began *The Death of Tragedy*. These were followed by a volume of three novellas, *Anno Domini*, and *Language and Silence*. He returned to England in 1961. His many honors include an O. Henry Short Story award, Fulbright and Guggenheim Fellowships, and the first award of the Morton Zabel Prize by the National Institute of Arts and Letters in 1970. He is married, with two children. He is at present engaged on a full-scale study of the poetics and linguistics of multilingualism and of translation.